CLEEVE HILL

The History of the Common and its People

John S[...]
Mail Order
Feb '97

For my parents, Vera and Clifford Aldred

*One rarely finds any reference to Commons and
Common Rights in the index of even the most
erudite social and economic histories.*

L.D. Stamp and W.G. Hoskins
The Common Lands of England and Wales, *1963*

CLEEVE HILL
The History of the Common and its People

DAVID H. ALDRED

ALAN SUTTON

First published in the United Kingdom in 1990 by
Alan Sutton Publishing Limited · Phoenix Mill · Far Thrupp · Stroud
Gloucestershire

First published in the United States of America in 1991 by
Alan Sutton Publishing Inc · Wolfeboro Falls · NH 03896–0848

British Library Cataloguing in Publication Data

Aldred, David H.
Cleeve Hill.
1. England. Common Land.
I. Title
333.2

ISBN 0–86299–827–1

Library of Congress Cataloging in Publication Data
Aldred, David H.
The history of Cleeve Hill / David H. Aldred.
p.   cm.
"First published in the United Kingdom in 1990 by Alan Sutton Publishing Ltd.
. . ."–T.p. verso.
Includes bibliographical references (p.   ) and index.
ISBN 0–86299–827–1 : $18.00
1. Commons–England–Cleeve Hill–History.   2. Cleeve Hill (England)–
History.   I. Title.
HD1289.G7A74   1991
333.2–dc20   90–46755
                                                          CIP

Cover picture: Visitors to the 'Cotswold Health Resort': A photograph taken at
the top of Stockwell Lane in the opening years of the twentieth century.

Typeset in 10/11pt Sabon.
Typesetting and origination by
Alan Sutton Publishing Limited.
Printed in Great Britain by
Dotesios Printers Limited.

Contents

Cleeve Hill: the common and its people in 1964. A view taken from the south-west. Many features visible here are discussed throughout the book [Hunting Aero Films]

Preface

This book tells the story of a landscape and of the people who have played a part in its creation. Cleeve Hill lies some four miles north-east of Cheltenham in Gloucestershire. It reaches a height of 1,083 ft (330 m) – the highest point of the Cotswolds – and is considered, technically, a mountain. Rising out of the Severn Vale its common of over one thousand acres can be seen for miles. It not only shelters the vale physically from the east but also metaphorically provides a backcloth to the lives of the people who live and work at its feet.

Cleeve Hill has fascinated me for most of my life, and yet when I began to investigate its past I found very little had been written about it. As L.D. Stamp and W.G. Hoskins noted in 1963, common land has not attracted much attention from historians or historical geographers. Although written nearly thirty years ago their statement still has validity. This book is intended in some small way to add to our limited knowledge of the subject.

The aim is not only to explain the development of a human landscape as I interpret the evidence, but also to explain how the landscape itself can be read for the clues to its own past. It is a book to read at home and take on walks over the hill. It is a book of local interest and yet it should have a wider value to students of landscape history, and the general reader, as a rare example of a full length history of an extensive area of common pasture. To this purpose I have borne in mind the need at all times to set the history of the hill into its wider contexts, for only in such contexts can its history be fully understood. Local history must not become parochial history.

I have arranged the chapters around themes. The general themes of conflict, continuity and change link with the more detailed themes of grazing, quarrying, woodland and settlement. The choice of themes is necessarily subjective but they seem to me to provide the best structure for arranging the evidence to give coherence to the history and prevent its fragmenting into a series of unrelated episodes.

In order to keep the story flowing, I have chosen a number of conventions that need some explanation here. Footnotes have been replaced by a section on further reading at the end of each chapter. Acknowledgements for the illustrations have been included in the captions. Where none appears the illustrations are my own. I have generally kept the historic measurements as they were used at the time. Readers not totally familiar with such measurements, or their metric equivalents, might wish to know that 1 mile = 1.6 km; 1 acre = 0.4 hectare; 240d. = 20s. = £1 = 100p.

As any author will acknowledge, such pieces of research would not be possible without the generous help and cooperation of many people. I am pleased to make those acknowledgements either in the captions or at the end of the book. However, a special acknowledgement needs to made here. In 1958 my parents made a decision to move us from Manchester to Woodmancote. Without that decision I would never have come to know Cleeve Hill and this book would never have been written. It seems appropriate, therefore, to dedicate this book to them.

David H. Aldred
November 1990

Introduction

Common land is any land over which there are rights of common.
B. Harris and G. Ryan, *An outline law relating to Common Land*, 1967

This history seeks to explain the development of the landscape of Cleeve Hill in general, and the history of its common in particular. The history of such common land has been strangely neglected. This is in part accounted for by the perception of common land as waste land with little value except for animal grazing. It is also accounted for by the lack of any identifiable

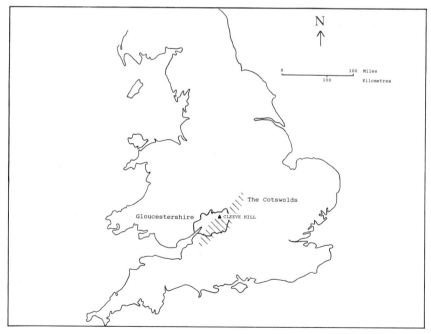

Location map of Cleeve Hill

body of records on which a study can be based. Arable land grew lifegiving crops; people needed to know who held which land and so many records were created over a long period of time. On the other hand common pasture generated few records and in many places all traces of such land have disappeared, leaving areas like Cleeve as lucky survivors. Readers have only to turn to the 'Further Reading' section of each chapter to confirm the lack of any single body of relevant records. Yet the failure to study common pasture belittles its importance, not only as part of a traditional pre-industrial economy, but also, more recently, as land for recreation and relaxation away from modern urban life. Just the fact that Cleeve Common has survived until the present is testimony to its value in a variety of contexts, and its future as a protected open space is now assured.

Cleeve Common was created by the coming together of two separate forces for change in the landscape: the natural geology and geomorphology, and the work of human beings. This chapter sets the scene by discussing both these forces, starting with the natural.

Cleeve Hill was formed around 180 million years ago as the sea bed of a shallow sea, created from shells, corals and carbonate of lime. Then the land was folded upwards, higher in the west than in the east, to create that famous scarp which today runs from Bath to Chipping Campden with its gentle dip slope stretching eastwards as the Cotswolds. The scarp is gradually being eroded towards the east, cut into by fast flowing streams on their way to the vale to reach the Severn. The process is continuous but barely discernible. It will, in time, separate Cleeve from Nottingham Hills, and leave the latter a true outlier like Langley or more distant Bredon. The erosive power of water can be seen on the common itself which is now cut by the northward facing valleys of Dry Bottom and Watery Bottom.

This timescale is slow beyond comprehension, but the recorded human story has been affected by the underlying geology in significant ways. The limestone, called Inferior Oolite, has been exploited for centuries: the smooth, good quality freestone for building material; coarser limestones, the peagrits and ragstones, for field walls, roadstone and lime for mortar; and sand, gravel and grits, which have been extracted for a variety of purposes, from creating footpaths to polishing marble. The exploitation of these minerals for over two thousand years clearly changed the appearance of the common and created its famous outline as seen from the vale.

The limestone itself soaks up the rainfall and results in a quick-drying surface which, in combination with continued animal grazing, has inhibited regeneration of trees after their original clearance and in more recent times has provided good turf for horse racing and training. However, in places bands of clay lie between the limestone beds. Here the water cannot pass, and so it emerges as a spring – the one in Watery Bottom above the Washpool is a good example. In other places the clay becomes waterlogged and slumps down the slope. This accounts for the instability of the land

Falling railings provide clear evidence of land slippage along the B4632

bordering the B4632, and has caused great problems for builders, house-holders and the highway authorities. The slumping created a ledge running along the slope which provided a convenient route for the present road when it was laid in 1823. Collapsed walls and twisted railings which line the road today provide the visual evidence for the potential instability of the ground.

The geology has provided the people with the opportunity to exploit and develop a natural resource. What use have they made of it?

The proper answer to that question forms the content of this book, but here it is necessary to consider the nature of common land, for there are many misconceptions about it, and the quotation at the beginning of this chapter indicates clearly the problem of finding a meaningful definition.

Two popular misconceptions concern common land: that it is not owned by anybody, and that everybody has rights to it. Common land has historically been part of the manorial waste and therefore belonged to whomsoever was Lord of the Manor. This is still the situation on Cleeve but in many places local authorities have bought commons, especially near large centres of population, to ensure free access. Traditionally, rights to the use of common land have been limited to commoners – people of the manor with land in the manor, who have used the land and its produce for animal

The familiar notices at the main entrances summarize the uses of the common as laid down by the 1890 regulation act. The trainers' notice provides a continuing link between the common and horse racing

grazing, firewood, turf or peat collection, and in certain places for grazing pigs in woodland. Rights of way and then increased access for others to enjoy the open spaces became established by usage over the years. In the case of Cleeve, Cheltenham Corporation has paid an annual sum since 1890 to allow its inhabitants rights of access and recreation. In theory there is no universal right of access; in practice the attraction of the common is the freedom to roam across it almost at will. Many of the major struggles to preserve commons in the nineteenth century concerned attempts to keep open the access to common land around London at places like Epping Forest, Hampstead Heath and Berkhampsted. These struggles in turn led to the setting up in 1865 of the Commons, Open Spaces and Footpaths Preservation Society to bring pressure for legislation. The most important piece of legislation resulting from this pressure was the 1876 Commons Act which allowed uses of any common to be regulated by law, if requested by a sufficient number of people. By 1914 thirty-six applications had been made under the act, one of which was for Cleeve. The details of this can be read in Chapter Five.

The general concern for the preservation of commons in the nineteenth century clearly reflected the threat they were perceived to be under. There are approximately one and a half million acres surviving in England and Wales today; between 1845 and 1869 over six hundred thousand acres were enclosed and taken into private ownership. Cleeve Common extends to over thirteen hundred acres and remains the largest in Gloucestershire. That it has survived was largely the result of the large number of people who were insistent on their rights of common at enclosure of the open fields in 1847. Many other local commons were subdivided and subsequently ploughed as a result of similar enclosure. This happened to the common on Nottingham Hill with the enclosure of Gotherington in 1807, and Prestbury and Sevenhampton's share of Cleeve Down disappeared as common land at their enclosure in 1732 and 1811 respectively. Written records indicate how relatively easy it is for us to trace the disappearance, or the survival, of common land with reasonable certainty. Conversely they remind us how difficult it is to trace the origins of common and waste land. This is one of the subjects the early part of the book attempts to investigate in relation to Cleeve, but what can be said more generally about their origin?

There is no clear date by which commons could be said to have come into existence. One of the problems facing historians is that the type of land most frequently described today as common land is, strictly speaking, common pasture. The arable open fields were common fields because the tenants had rights over them, for example the right to graze their animals on the fallow fields. Parliamentary enclosure of the eighteenth and nineteenth centuries was usually the last stage of the conversion into private property as the fields we know today. Other types of land use could also be held in common: Tewkesbury Ham is still a common meadow today; the name Sherwood is a reminder that Sherwood Forest was centred on a wood in which the people of Nottinghamshire had woodland rights, first recorded in AD 958.

Another problem concerns the nature of the record. It has so far been impossible to recognize common land from archaeological evidence and it could have been held in common long before the first written recordings, which might have been made only when the rights were under threat. However, there is clear evidence that the concept of common grazing land predated the Norman Conquest. Stamp and Hoskins record that by the early thirteenth century Dartmoor provided common grazing for the whole of Devon, except for the boroughs of Barnstaple and Totnes which were founded in the mid-tenth century, presumably after the time by which the rights to Dartmoor had become established. The earliest date we possess for common grazing on Cleeve is 1150 (see Chapter Three).

In theory the uses of common land have been controlled by custom and byelaw. Traditionally this was the work of the manor court. Much of this

Sheep grazing on the common provide a constant theme which links the present with the past. A postcard view taken earlier this century

book is concerned with such cases. Probably the greatest need to control usage has been to prevent overgrazing, by limiting the number of animals any one person could turn out on to the common pasture. This was known as 'stinting'. It first appears when records became generally available in the early thirteenth century, and probably reflected a growth of pressure on common lands throughout England. At different times and in different places different figures were employed to regulate stinting. There were attempts to stint Cleeve Common on several occasions in the past – such repetition being a clear indication that the stints were not being observed.

Common pasture developed and retained its importance when tenants had insufficient land on their holding to pasture enough animals to keep it manured, particularly in the growing season when only the fallow field was available. In Bishop's Cleeve the typical size of holding was thirty acres during the later Middle Ages. Anything which prevented the commoners from enjoying their rights was considered anti-community, particularly encroachment on to the common. This led to parts of it being enclosed for private use. The traditional belief that the builders of a house constructed overnight with smoke issuing from the chimney by morning could claim squatters' rights probably explains encroachment on the edges of Cleeve

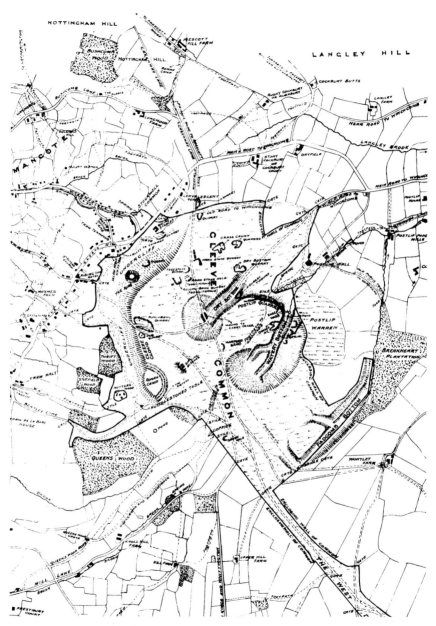

Dr J.H. Garrett's map, drawn to accompany *From A Cotswold Height* (1919), still remains a useful guide to the common and its approaches [J.V. Garrett]

Common. The manorial courts had varying success in removing such enclosures from the late-seventeenth century onwards.

The history of Cleeve Common reflects the general trends which have affected common pasture throughout the country. However, its continued existence – with little change to its boundaries for over a thousand years – singles it out as worthy of attention.

FURTHER READING

The most readable account of the underlying geology of Cleeve Hill and the Cotswolds is *Geology explained in the Severn Vale and Cotswolds*, by W. Dreghorn (David & Charles, Newton Abbot, 1967). The most detailed and scholarly is still *A Handbook of the Geology of Cheltenham and Neighbourhood*, by L. Richardson (Norman, Sawyer & Co., Cheltenham, 1904).

For commons in general the standard reference work is *The Common Lands of England and Wales* by L.D. Stamp and W.G. Hoskins (Collins, London, 1963). *Common Land and Enclosure* by E.C.K. Gonner (1912; reprinted by F. Cass, London, 1966) is only for the committed. *English Commons and Forests* by G. Shaw-Le Fèvre (Cassell, London, 1894) traces the development of the fight to preserve commons in the nineteenth century, and is written by a founder member of the Commons, Open Spaces and Footpaths Preservation Society. *The Common Land Forum Report* (Cheltenham, 1986) was produced by the Countryside Commission for England and Wales to make recommendations on the future management of commons. It includes much of general interest.

Gloucestershire Commons: Their History, Wildlife and Future (Gloucestershire Trust for Nature Conservancy, Stonehouse, 1989) provides a useful summary of the county's commons. Many local historical studies make incidental references to commons and wastes. The Victoria County History of Gloucestershire, which is slowly covering the county's parishes, often includes relevant references in its sections entitled 'Economic History', which are included in every parish study. The county common closest to Cleeve in its form and functions is at Minchinhampton, dealt with in *Minchinhampton and Avening* by A.T. Playne (1915; reprinted by Alan Sutton Publishing, Gloucester, 1978). There are many books on the Forest of Dean. Those by Dr Cyril Hart cover its history, but the position of common land in the Forest is altogether different from Cleeve Common.

Two books have been written on Cleeve Common. The best known is *From a Cotswold Height* by Dr J.H. Garrett (J.J. Banks, Cheltenham, 1919; reprinted by Alan Sutton Publishing, Gloucester, 1988) which describes a series of walks made over and around the common in the early years of the century. Unfortunately for the historian the best descriptions are those of the area's natural history, which has since changed rather less than its social and economic history. Readers interested in this aspect of the common should refer to Dr Garrett's book for a comprehensive treatment of a subject not covered here. *Cleeve Common, Glos., Rights and Regulations over this Common*, by J.F. Daubeny (Army & Navy Cooperative Society, London, 1900) consists mostly of legal clauses, as it was an attempt to clarify the legal obligations of the then Lady of the Manor *vis-à-vis* the powers of the Conservators. It does, however, contain some useful, if incidental, contemporary information.

The history of Cleeve Hill and its common is discussed briefly in 'When Cleeve ceased to be common' in *Gloucestershire and Avon Life* (D.H. Aldred, October, 1977). Sections of two books in Alan Sutton Publishing's 'The British Isles in Old Photographs' series contain many postcard and other views of the common at the turn of the century; they are *Bishop's Cleeve to Winchcombe in Old Photographs* (1987) and *Around Bishop's Cleeve and Winchcombe in Old Photographs* (1989). There is to date no full history of the hill and its common available, which gives the main reason for writing this book.

CHAPTER ONE

The Making of the Human Landscape (before *c.* AD 400)

Before, however, entering on the authenticated incidents recorded of the eighth century, it will be interesting to trace back, briefly, (so far as is practicable through so long a vista of remote ages) some of the facts presented to us by the discoveries of ancient British and Roman remains.

E. Dent, *The Annals of Winchcombe and Sudeley,* 1877

Some Early Problems

Every story has a beginning. Emma Dent quite clearly believed that her story began with 'the authenticated incidents recorded of the eighth century'. More than a hundred years of archaeological research have yielded much knowledge of prehistory so that it now deserves greater mention than a footnote attached to a story based largely on the written word, but our knowledge is still incomplete. Understanding still depends upon recognition and interpretation of fragmentary pieces of evidence, and parallels which can never provide conclusive answers. For this reason the first few millenia of Cleeve Hill's history require no more space than a single chapter, while the rest of the book is taken up with developments since AD 400.

Prehistory is divided conventionally into different ages. These are simple conveniences for the prehistorian and archaeologist, but they do give a structure to the early part of the story and will be used here to that purpose. By following chronological divisions it is easier to identify the recurring themes which are echoed in the area's later history.

The basis of this chapter is the evidence of the landscape itself – there are no written records to support its interpretation. But the landscape yields its clues only grudgingly and has to be handled with care. Knowledge of the hill's history has emerged from a small number of actual excavations, dating back to 1863; from careful examination of surviving features; and from stray finds, which were reported and recorded. This type of information creates two major problems: firstly, how should this material be interpreted in order to look behind the feature to the people who made it, and moulded the landscape? Secondly, how typical are the features which survive? How accurate is the picture we can paint from necessarily fragmentary and incomplete evidence? These considerations need to be kept in mind, but they must not be allowed to undermine the conclusion that the evidence quite clearly points to prehistory as the period in which the present general features of Cleeve Hill and its common were formed.

The First Clearances

No evidence has yet been found for human activity on the hill before the final retreat of the glaciers in the last Ice Age over twelve thousand years ago. They had stretched down to the Bredon Hill area, and as the weather warmed the countryside became colonized by birch and pine, then hazel and oak with lesser numbers of elm and lime. There are some indications that trees were being cleared, at least on a small scale, from *c.* 4000 BC. Most of the evidence for this mesolithic period which has been found on the Cotswolds has come from scatters of flint picked up from walking across ploughed fields. Flint does not occur naturally on the Cotswolds and its discovery must indicate human presence. Such opportunities for field walking are very limited on Cleeve but the archaeological investigation of Haymes Romano-British settlement (see page 15) did uncover three flints which could be dated to the mesolithic period. Their significance is unclear, except that they indicate some form of human activity at that distant date on land that was no longer completely wooded. Further evidence may lie under the predominantly pastoral land use of the common and its surrounding fields.

The earliest period for which there is more than fragmentary evidence in the landscape is the neolithic period, when farming was first introduced into the area. A burial mound *under* Belas Knap long barrow dates from *c.* 3500 BC, which provides a date by which people were living in the area and clearing the landscape. Belas Knap is one of the best known of some sixty long barrows in Gloucestershire and has been excavated at least twice, between 1863 and 1865, and again between 1928 and 1930. The present impressive monument is largely a reconstruction done after the last excavation. Although it is no longer possible to accept the hypothesis put forward by Dr Grundy in *Saxon Charters and Fieldnames of Gloucestershire* (1935) in his attempt to identify the boundaries of the *Timbingctun* estate, for reasons which are discussed in the next chapter, its proximity to the common does allow us to draw some conclusions about Cleeve over five thousand years ago.

It is well known that long barrows were communal graves. Thirty-eight

Burrow's sketch of Belas Knap of 1913 shows the extent of the modern reconstruction after the excavations of 1928–30

skeletons were identified from the bones lying in Belas Knap's four chambers, but why should such a large construction be built over such a small burial area (less than 5 per cent of the total area), and why only thirty-eight skeletons in its period of use which possibly stretched from *c.* 3000 BC to *c.* 2500 BC? There is no conclusive answer to these questions whether directed at Belas Knap in particular or long barrows in general, but the most recent theories suggest that they should be viewed as repositories for the bones of the ancestors used to legitimize a people's right to their land, and as territorial markers. So how can this help in attempting to reconstruct the development of the landscape on Cleeve Hill?

In the early 1980s Alan Saville excavated a long barrow at Hazleton near Northleach. He showed it had been built in a sizeable woodland clearing. The situation at Belas Knap seems to have been very similar. Field walking has produced flint scatters across the plateau which extends to Cleeve Common and Wontley. Pieces of flint sickle blades and a flint saw were found inside the tombs. Fragments of pottery indicated storage and preparation of food. Animals were represented by bones of horse and pig; the latter suggesting (controlled) use of woodland for hunting, or pasture for domesticated breeds. Woodland remained uncleared on the scarp faces longer than in other areas, but by 2500 BC, when Belas Knap appears to have gone out of use, the high plateau had already been cleared of woodland

and Cleeve Hill was developing its open aspect. How far did the clearances extend?

Scatters of worked flint picked up between the edge of the common and Wontley suggest that it might be only the present pasture use of the common which prevents us picking up flints from across the common itself. This idea is further supported by two other known scatters of flint. The excavations at the King's Beeches in 1902 (see page 10) recovered three flints and further investigation towards the Stables Quarry produced a few more. More spectacularly, sixty-seven flints had been retrieved at Haymes Romano-British settlement site by 1985, indicating activity in the neolithic period following on (although not necessarily continuously) from the earlier mesolithic period at this place. These flints would support the conclusion that clearance was primarily for arable farming, and that continuity of land use as arable or possibly, later, as pasture made it difficult for trees to re-establish themselves. It could be that use as pasture followed only after exhaustion of the soil by arable farming, as happened on other upland areas such as Dartmoor or on the chalk downlands of southern England at the end of the Bronze Age. However, we know from the excavations of Belas Knap from 1863 to 1865 that quantities of Iron Age and Romano-British pottery were found adjacent to the site. This could suggest a movement back to arable use by c. 500 BC, for the sherds of pottery came with the manure from the farmyard, possibly indicating a farm occupied for only part of the

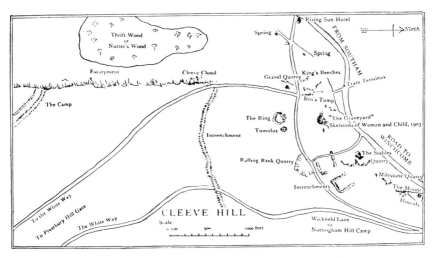

This sketch map drawn to accompany G.W.S. Brewer's report on his excavations at the King's Beeches provides a valuable, if impressionistic, record of the archaeological features on the common in 1904

year when the animals grazed on the upland; another feature identified from excavated sites in the south and west of England.

We know more about how the landscape changed in the neolithic period than about the people responsible for the changes. No evidence of settlement has been found on the hill. This could be due to five millennia of erosion which have removed the soil carrying the evidence of timber buildings. Some probably lived in the vale, where centuries of cultivation and exploitation of the land have destroyed the evidence. Stray finds of flints suggest the vale itself had large clearings by at least 2000 BC. The vale looks up to Cleeve Hill but no clear evidence of a long barrow as a territorial marker visible from the vale is known to exist. The long mound known as 'Ben's Tump', which lies on the common above the Rising Sun, could be a long barrow. In the nineteenth century some 'ancient' pottery was found near it, but this is hardly conclusive. Only excavation will be able to establish whether it is a natural feature or man-made. Thus there is a lack of any clear evidence that the hill had yet become attached to any developing territory in the vale.

The Landscape Takes its Present Form

It is impossible to consider any of these prehistoric periods in any detail; one can only hope to identify trends in the development of the landscape. Belas Knap was deliberately abandoned approximately as the neolithic period merged into the Bronze Age in *c.* 2500 BC. People continued to exploit the potential of the hill, however. During the neolithic period and the Bronze Age the climate was significantly warmer than that of today, thus making life at the higher altitude of Cleeve rather more hospitable for growing crops and living there. Most of the evidence we possess has come from grave goods, buried with the people to serve them in the next world, from a number of known round barrows. These were scattered when the barrows were destroyed: few, if any, barrows still survive. The greater number of round barrows than of long barrows suggests an increase in population and groups were competing for land; some three hundred round barrows are known to have existed in Gloucestershire. They might well also have been territorial markers, placed on the margins of cultivated land to proclaim ownership. The round barrows on Cleeve were placed to be visible from the vale, and they thus provide the first evidence that the western face of the hill had been claimed by the adjacent parts of the vale. Was this territory a precursor of the ancient parish?

Readers familiar with the large numbers of well-preserved round barrows on the Wiltshire Downs will be disappointed with their evidence on Cleeve. Only one structure remotely looks like a barrow today – the round platform adjacent to 'The Ring' earthwork, east of Rising Sun Lane. Although it was

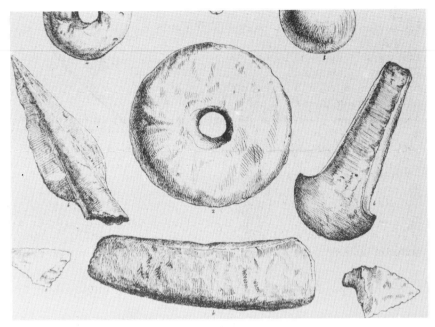

Two bronze axes and a spearhead (marked '6') found on Cleeve Hill and illustrated in Emma Dent's *The Annals of Winchcombe and Sudeley* (1877)

recorded in 1884 on the first large scale Ordnance Survey map as a round barrow, the 1976 inventory of the Royal Commission on Historical Monuments (RCHM) described it as the possible site of a later Iron Age hut. Only careful excavation will throw further light on the matter. Two low mounds barely 2 ft in height near the radio masts on West Down have also been identified as round barrows. Again the existing evidence is inconclusive. Most of our knowledge of the round barrows, therefore, comes from the writings of earlier historians.

In 1779 Samuel Rudder recorded four barrows lying equidistant between Nottingham Hill and Cleeve Hill camps. One had recently been opened to yield a large quantity of human bones, 'broken and crumbled'. John Goding's *Norman's History of Cheltenham*, written in 1863, made further reference to them, and they were obviously still visible in *c.* 1903 when amateur archaeologist G.W.S. Brewer picked up scattered bones, and recorded them on a map as 'mounds' (see page 4). At this latter date the barrows were being destroyed by the expansion of Milestone Quarry. It is just possible the most southerly barrow still survives as a low mound,

Milestone Quarry as it appears today. The low mound on the skyline, between the wall and a larger mound, may be the last of the round barrows recorded in 1904 [T.N. Curr]

although it is now covered by more recent debris. Some of the stray finds made during the nineteenth century (and now in Cheltenham Museum) might have come from these barrows. The finds included several bronze axes, a miniature dagger and what is probably a large-socketed axe. Their use could have been ceremonial rather than practical. In 1931 a little known find of pottery and bones, said to have been those of an old woman, was made by workmen digging for water pipes where the public conveniences have now been built at the top of Stockwell Lane. This could have been another Bronze Age, or possible Iron Age, burial.

Further evidence for activity in the Bronze Age has been found on Nottingham Hill. In his introduction to the *Landboc* of Winchcombe Abbey, published in 1892, the Revd David Royce referred to three round barrows on the hill. No trace can be found of them today, but in 1972 ploughing within the site of the Iron Age camp disturbed a hoard of twenty-five Bronze Age objects hidden in a wooden box, including three bronze swords. Now in Cheltenham Museum, they provide evidence not only that the hill had been cleared of woodland by the late Bronze Age, after *c.* 1000 BC, but also of possible occupation *before* the development of the hillfort.

There was much activity on Cleeve Hill in the Bronze Age. By *c.* 700 BC the countryside was probably open and exploited both on the hilltop

Nottingham Hill hillfort showing the ramparts in the foreground and Granna (or Grinnell) Lane cutting across the plateau. Until enclosure in 1807 this area, like Cleeve, was common pasture [Cambridge University Collection: copyright reserved]

plateau and in the vale. People moved around in the landscape. Tin and copper came from the south-west; flint from the south-east; people drove animals to and from pastures. Many of the routes marked on the map on page 32 were probably in use during the Bronze Age, particularly the route coming up Nottingham Hill as Granna or Grinnell Lane and across Cleeve as the White Way before forking, the south-eastern route following West Down and the more southerly route passing on to Ham Hill and through Dowdeswell. Although the evidence for use of all the routes from the vale up the scarp is clearer for the Iron Age, it is unlikely they were new creations in that period, for Cleeve Hill had already become a scarce resource. Timothy Darvill, one of the country's leading archaeologists, has suggested that the ditch and bank running across the hill to Dry Bottom and Postlip Quarries, which later became the manorial boundary, date from the Bronze Age rather than the Iron Age as previously thought. From parallels elsewhere, particularly Icomb Hill near Stow-on-the-Wold, he considers it divided the area into two territories. Thus by the end of the Bronze Age c. 700 BC the landscape was filling and boundaries needed to be clearer. If this was the

The linear ditch, which Timothy Darvill considers may date from the Bronze Age, seen here near the Trig Point [T.N. Curr]

case, Cleeve and much of its later common already lay in the territory of the settlements in the vale. With its limestone barrows standing in open pasture and visible for miles and with a ditch running up from what is now Rising Sun Lane, it must have formed an impressive landscape, but one which quite clearly belonged to the territory directly at the bottom of the scarp; not to Prestbury nor over the dip slope to Charlton Abbots, Sevenhampton, Sudeley or Winchcombe although there could well have been shared rights to the pasture and woodland during the next fifteen hundred years (see Chapter Two). By *c*. 700 BC we could say that the forerunner of Cleeve had successfully staked its claim to its hill.

The First Settlements

It may be hypothesized that by the early Iron Age Cleeve Hill became an open pasture attached to the later territory of Cleeve. We have no knowledge of where the people actually lived, nor of the rights and uses

Iron Age pottery from Cleeve Hill [Cheltenham Museum]

linked to the pasture, although it is possible to interpret the rectangular enclosures covering one and a half acres, between the golf club and the Stables Quarry, as stock controlling enclosures of the Bronze Age. With the unfolding of the Iron Age, however, there appears the first direct evidence of people living on the hill. That evidence comes from an archaeological dig at the King's Beeches undertaken in 1902 when gravel digging cut into a settlement platform. This reveals some clear evidence about life on Cleeve during the Iron Age.

It was clearly a place where pottery was made. A number of pits contained clay and shaped stones for fashioning pots, in addition to finished pottery. The pottery has been dated to between the sixth century BC and the first century AD. Some pieces have been identified as Severn–Avon valley ware, continuing links with the vale and further afield. Post holes and fragments of daub indicated wooden structures had been built there, but there was no evidence of fortification. Other finds suggested the type of economy that had existed then and, by implication, the nature of the landscape. Many sheep bones were found including a high proportion of bones from lambs, suggesting they were kept for food. They would have grazed on the upland pasture. Numerous pig bones were discovered; many of these were from young pigs, which again suggested domesticated animals, and nearby woodland for their pannage. Shells from a woodland species of snail confirmed that woodland must have been close at hand for snails do not travel far, even during a full, natural lifespan. There was indirect evidence that the settlers possessed dogs from the gnaw marks on many bones, but direct evidence was limited to only one bone and two teeth. Similarly the only evidence for arable farming was indirect – the remains of cattle teeth which could have indicated plough oxen. Although the remains of a horse were found it is more likely to have been for riding than hauling. Here, then, was a small settled community, at the junction of the pasture and woodland, dependent on farming but still hunting on occasions, for the remains of red and roe deer were also found. All the finds were sealed by quarry waste which contained three Roman *denarii* minted in London in AD 293. Not only do they tell us a date by which the settlement had been abandoned, but give us the earliest evidence for quarrying on the hill, possibly connected to the site at Haymes.

When the site was excavated by G.W.S. Brewer, he also noted other Iron Age finds which he included on his map. Unfortunately we know nothing about 'The Graveyard' but Iron Age finds from 'The Stables Quarry' were placed in Cheltenham Museum where they later became unfortunately mixed up with the finds from the King's Beeches. The pottery was very similar, indicating a contemporary date. The site was also undefined, possibly extending to the platform fifty metres to the south where more Iron Age, and also Romano-British, pottery was picked up in 1972 when a water pipe cut across its south-west corner. We can imagine here another small settlement consisting of a few timber-built huts with thatched roofs sitting in the landscape rather than dominating it, but farming it in a way not unfamiliar today. The earthwork known as 'The Ring' (clearly visible in the aerial photograph at the front of this book) could have been built in this period to control animals. Its actual presence confirms the use of the common as pasture at the time that it was built. All the possible Iron Age monuments on the hill have been examined in the RCHM's *Inventory* on Iron Age and Romano-British monuments in the Gloucestershire Cotswolds, which appeared in 1976. This volume gives a useful summary of knowledge about the period as it stood in the mid-1970s.

General awareness of the Iron Age is dominated by hillforts. Some thirty-five are spread along the Cotswold scarp from Bath to Chipping Campden; two of them lie in our area of study; none of them has been examined in detail. It is therefore necessary to turn to parallels, especially Crickley Hill to the south of Cheltenham, where annual excavations have taken place since 1969. At Nutterswood the hillfort as it can be seen today encloses three acres, although its original size is not known because it has been destroyed by quarrying. As late as 1779 Samuel Rudder was able to record an entrance fronting the scarp edge which has now gone. Comparison with Crickley would suggest an early Iron Age hillfort, dating from

Cleeve Cloud hillfort showing clearly the extent of damage by quarrying. The large circular feature near the edge is probably the remains of an enclosure constructed to protect saplings. The hamlet of Nutterswood appears at the bottom, and the wall of the common follows the Saxon charter boundary cutting across the top right-hand corner [Cambridge University Collection: copyright reserved]

The ramparts of Nottingham Hill hillfort, sketched in 1913 before they became covered with undergrowth

before *c.* 400 BC, with a single bank and ditch, developed into a double bank and ditch two or three centuries later. Two sherds of pottery confirm its existence at least between 700 BC and 500 BC. What was its purpose? Again by reference to Crickley, it was built to dominate, possibly a high status site for a social leader looking over his territory in the vale, from where the grain was brought up to feed the inhabitants of the hillfort. This would have been possible as a result of the landscape and territorial developments of the Bronze Age. The evidence is now conclusive that hill and vale were linked and that the hill had become a valuable resource, to be protected and defended against outside interests – one of the major themes of its history.

What of the other hillfort on Nottingham Hill, the scene of the burial of the Bronze Age hoard? Timothy Darvill considers it to have been an early Iron Age hilltop enclosure built for storing produce and keeping animals. The excavation of 1972 discovered a hearth and storage pits which indicated some habitation also. Its size of one hundred and twenty acres makes it a different type of hillfort to Cleeve and the two were possibly complementary rather than in the occupation of rival leaders. If the parallel with Crickley holds strong, then these hillforts would have gone out of use by *c.* 400 BC. The reasons for this change are unclear, except that around this time the large fortified hillforts such as Uley Bury and Salmonsbury

Modern development along Stockwell Lane easily masks its sunken nature

camp at Bourton-on-the-Water were developed, possibly suggesting the development of a more hierarchical society, with leaders controlling ever increasing territories leading ultimately to the emergence of the Dobunni in *c.* 100 BC, with their centre at Bagenden near Cirencester. The territory of Cleeve, never isolated from other areas in Britain, became increasingly integrated into a wider political world. Throughout the history of Cleeve Hill this wider context cannot be ignored.

The abandonment of the hillforts probably had little impact on the landscape of Cleeve Hill. The land uses had already been established, and the rather later dates for the abandonment of the undefended settlements suggests people might have moved to them for a time or consolidated around the settlements in the vale. Several of the latter have been discovered in recent years, particularly the large middle-Iron Age to Romano-British period site excavated in 1989 at Gilder's corner in Bishop's Cleeve. It is probably not just coincidence that Stockwell Lane forms a direct link between this site and the Stables Quarry site. There are steep holloways linking known sites in the vale to known sites on the scarp top along the whole of the Cotswold edge. The map on page 32 attempts to show this for the area of Cleeve Hill. Some tracks were probably local, but others more long distance, such as Granna Lane, or perhaps linked with crossings of the

Severn south of Tewkesbury. They support the hypothesis that the hill was used for animal pasture in this period, as the constant traffic caused the surface of these routes to lie lower than the surrounding ground level in places. The linkage of vale and hill is supported by archaeological finds at nearby Beckford in the vale where excavations have produced first-century BC pottery exactly the same as that found in the hillfort on Bredon Hill. Only excavation of the Cleeve Cloud hillfort will confirm this as a parallel here.

The Iron Age was an interlude of perhaps six centuries when continuity of land use and landscape appearance remained stable. The continuing similar needs of farmers possessed of similar technologies would not have changed the landscape dramatically. Elites probably developed and organized the building of the hillforts, which were occupied and then abandoned over perhaps no more than four hundred years. This does suggest, however, an intensifying competition for territories and their attendant rights to the land which seems to have emerged in the Bronze Age and which continued in one form or another right down to the present day. They remind us that when this part of the territory of the Dobunni came under the influence of the invading Roman armies and became a distant part of the vast Roman Empire shortly after the invasion of Britain in AD 43, the landscape was already developed and its people settled.

The arrival of Roman influences cannot be traced from the archaeological record. Iron Age pottery and timber buildings continued to be produced and only slowly did the population accept Roman ideas. In fact, some of the 'Iron Age' pottery found on the hill could well date from the Roman period. It may be assumed that the appearance of the hill, pasture above and then areas of woodland rising out of a cultivated vale, changed little during the first centuries AD, although there might have been some regeneration of woodland on the scarp at the end of the period and into the early Saxon period, if parallels in other places are applicable.

Reference has already been made to some Romano-British features – the scatter of pottery near Belas Knap indicating cultivated land between there and Wontley; a few sherds near the Stables Quarry; and the three coins found at the King's Beeches giving evidence of quarrying at the end of the third century AD. It was suggested then that such quarrying might have been connected with the site at Haymes Farm, the only Roman period site known on the hill. It was first discovered in 1974 when a water pipeline cut through the upper part of Wiremead (see map on page 88), and completely destroyed in 1985 when the Severn–Trent Water Authority built a reservoir over the site. Between these dates the site was excavated by Bernard and Barbara Rawes, on whose observations the following conclusions are based.

The excavations presented a very confused picture because of the soil slumping which had taken place since the site had been abandoned. The evidence of coins indicated occupation from the early second century to the

The view looking eastward across the site of Haymes Romano-British settlement shortly before the building of the reservoir in 1985. The excavations took place in the middle distance

end of the fourth century AD, although the pottery suggested there might have been an Iron Age settlement there even before the Roman conquest. At first the houses seem to have been timber with thatched roofs, but enough stones were found to suggest that later buildings had low stone walls on which timber-framed buildings had been erected, and clay tiles replaced thatch. Eighteen brooches were found, probably indicating offerings to a household god, for a small altar was also discovered on the site.

All the evidence points to the existence of a farmstead, not unlike the many known to have covered the vale in the Roman period. Bernard Rawes likens the site at Haymes to that which he excavated at Tredington Rise, west of Bishop's Cleeve, brought to light during the construction of the M5 motorway over twenty years ago. There is no direct evidence for arable farming, but the surprisingly large number of animal bones suggest grazing on the open downland. Dogs were also well represented and were presumably used in sheep farming. Cattle and horses needed pasture, while the presence of pigs' bones, and fragments of bone from red and fallow deer confirm the existence of woodland – as we would expect, although the presence of flints suggests the actual site had been cleared for thousands of years. The farmstead was probably surrounded by small fields growing the necessary crops protected by fences and hedges.

The massive sill-stone excavated at Haymes in 1975, which Bernard Rawes felt might have been at the entrance to a shrine [B. Rawes and Cheltenham Museum]

The small settlement at Haymes was clearly later than the hillforts and lasted longer than the Iron Age settlements on the common. Are they connected? It is impossible to decide, unless we look at the development of estate boundaries and find some continuities of land holding as a unit based on these sites on the southern part of the hill. It is possible that the two separate estates known to have existed in the eighth century, the coming together of which was later reflected in the ancient ecclesiastical parish of Bishop's Cleeve, could have been the same territories. The creation of the sub-manor of Southam in the tenth century might also have reflected this prehistoric structure. However, the subsequent development of these territories as economic or political units can be traced only with difficulty, although the landscape itself passed through a long period of little change.

Some Continuing Problems

This chronological look at Cleeve Hill has enabled the limited evidence to be used to establish that by the Bronze Age at the latest the landscape of the hill

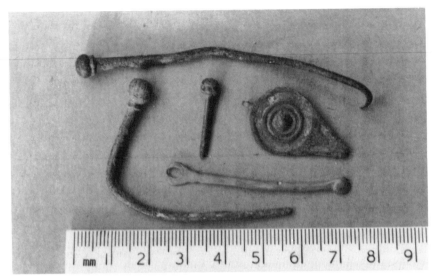

Bronze pins and a seal-box lid, some of the artefacts found at Haymes and now in
Cheltenham Museum [B. Rawes and Cheltenham Museum]

had largely taken its present form. It has also allowed the introduction of
the fundamental concepts underpinning this study: continuity, change and
conflict over a scarce economic resource. The major themes of land use,
settlement patterns and boundaries will be considered in more detail as the
evidence for them becomes more plentiful in studies of the succeeding
centuries.

Much of the discussion in this chapter has focused on the interpretation
of chance observations and finds. Only at Belas Knap, the King's Beeches
and Haymes has any serious archaeological research been carried out, and
the former two sites were investigated many years ago when techniques for
retrieving evidence were much less advanced than they are today. We have
knowledge of other finds made in the nineteenth century which are
potentially very significant, but which are now lost. In 1811 the *Cheltenham
Chronicle* reported the discovery of two large earthenware pots containing
gold and silver coins from the end of the fourth century AD at Cleeve,
presumably on the hill. Half a century later the *Gloucester Journal* recorded
the finding by quarrymen around the Nutterswood hillfort of 'soldiers'
graves', presumably skeletons in stone coffins, together with some coins
mostly dating from the reign of the third Caesar, plus burnt bones, the
foundations of a 'Roman dwelling' and some other relics which they sold to

strangers. This took place in 1863. Lord Ellenborough, the lord of Southam manor, stopped the quarrying to carry out a proper investigation but no later report has ever been discovered and the finds were lost. If the recording was accurate the finds could have indicated an early Roman presence, even possibly a military presence, for the third Caesar was Caligula (who died in AD 41), and the coin could have been brought as soldiers' pay in the early days of conquest following AD 43. Also in 1863 J. Goding's *Norman's History of Cheltenham* recorded the discovery of a Dobunnic coin, a lance head and a human skeleton during quarrying in the entrenchments of Nottingham Hill. No further record of these finds exists, but they do provide possible evidence for a reoccupation of the hillfort at the end of the Iron Age. However the most enigmatic and tantalizing reference to a feature which could be of immense significance, but which is now lost, is to the large figure of a horse carved on the scarp near the hillfort and visible from Cheltenham. We know of its existence from Emma Dent's account in the *Winchcombe and Sudeley Record* of March 1891. In the article she recounted how it had been cut to honour the visit of George III to Cheltenham in 1788; how a gang of labourers made an annual visit, starting with breakfast at the Rising Sun, to recut it; how this ceased in the 1840s; and how by 1866 the figure was fading and then destroyed by quarrying. Emma Dent however was an accurate recorder of events of her own life time, but a recounter of folk-myths as explanations, rather than a searcher after truth. Recent archaeological investigations on existing hill figures, especially the White Horse of Uffington, have shown conclusively how such figures were recut and refashioned over centuries. Careful investigation of Cheltenham Museum's archive on the 1788 royal visit has produced no confirmatory evidence that this was the origin of the figure. We know from coins that the horse was an important symbol for the Dobunni; was it they who originally cut such a figure cut here, near the Cleeve Cloud hillfort, as another territorial marker signifying the attachment of this area of the hill to its territory in the vale? In the light of available knowledge this cannot be discounted.

Of course it is possible that these and other finds, past and future, could force a modification of our present understanding of how the landscape of Cleeve Hill developed before the first written evidence of the late eighth century. However it is very unlikely to force a change in the view that by AD 400 the present appearance of the hill was largely complete.

FURTHER READING

Much of this chapter has been based upon my interpretation of a variety of archaeological reports, linking them to the present landscape as relevant. The best starting points for this period are undoubtedly Timothy Darvill's

Prehistoric Gloucestershire (Alan Sutton Publishing and Gloucestershire County Library, Gloucester, 1987) and Alan Saville (ed.), *Archaeology in Gloucestershire* (Cheltenham Art Gallery and Museums, and Bristol and Gloucestershire Archaeological Society, Cheltenham, 1984), which also have relevance for Chapters Two and Three. They both contain excellent bibliographies of more detailed works.

Many articles have been written in the *Transactions of the Bristol and Gloucestershire Archaeological Society*. The major articles used here have been from Volumes 51/2 (1929/30) on Belas Knap; Volume 96 (1978) on the Iron Age sites, and Volume 104 (1986) on Haymes. The report of the King's Beeches excavations can be found in the *Proceedings of the Cotteswold Naturalists' Field Club* Volume 15 (1904). Other useful references have been indicated in the main body of the text.

The main locations of the finds have been indicated in the text, although not all of them are on public display. The County Archaeologist at Shire Hall in Gloucester keeps an up-to-date gazetteer of all known sites in the county, which can be consulted by prior appointment.

CHAPTER TWO

The Boundaries are Defined
(*c.* AD 400–1086)

This syndon tha landgemaeru to Wendles Clife.
(These are the bounds of the Steep Slope of the Quarry into which
a Wagon Track runs.)
  G.B. Grundy, *Saxon Charters and Field Names of Gloucestershire,*
  part 1, 1935

Sources and Contexts

The six hundred years following the Roman occupation of the area are
important in the evolution of Cleeve Hill and its common, for it is during
this period that the boundaries of the common were first established, and
that its name was first recorded. In general, however, there is a lack of
evidence for the period between the decline of Roman Britain and Domesday, and it is necessary to use a broader context to understand more clearly
the changes, continuities and conflicts of the period.

The traditional view of the Anglo-Saxon invasions is of a people
slaughtering the remaining Romano-British population or driving them to
Wales and the West Country, taking over an empty landscape where they
built their villages and managed open fields, leaving the margins of their
territories as woodland and waste. They brought cataclysm and change into
the landscape. Superficially the development of the Cleeve area fits this
model. Many place-names undoubtedly date from the Saxon period –
Cleeve itself (at the cliff), Cockbury (Cocca's camp), Padcombe (Pata's
valley), Wontley (Honta's burial mound). The woodland lay away from the
arable on the scarp slopes, and the so-called waste, Cleeve Common, ran to
the territorial boundary. This follows a commonly accepted perception of
the period – but the reality was very different.

Recent work by archaeologists, historians and place-name scholars
suggests the Anglo-Saxon invasions led to a political takeover of an existing
population by a relatively small number of people. In places Romano-

British leaders, such as the legendary King Arthur, resisted the westward advance, but overall there was no mass slaughter, no resettlement of the existing population and no instant foundation of new villages. In Gloucester and Cirencester there is clear evidence of these Romano-British centres still existing as settlements long after the traditional end of the Roman period in 410, and being of enough significance to be recorded as falling to the Saxons after the Battle of Dyrham in 577.

Only a scant picture of Cleeve during this period can be provided by the limited archaeological evidence and historical context. One coin dated to *c*. 390, found by Bernard Rawes on the Haymes settlement site, provides us with a latest date for Romano-British occupation on the hill. In the 1960s a late sixth-century Saxon cemetery was excavated during gravel digging near Lower Farm just to the south of Bishop's Cleeve. Twenty-seven identifiable skeletons were recorded. They had been buried with pagan rites which indicated that the area had come under Anglo-Saxon influence by that date.

In 628 Penda, King of Mercia, led his army to victory over the army of Wessex at Cirencester to incorporate the area into Mercia. Until *c*. 800 Bishop's Cleeve lay in the sub-kingdom of the Hwicce. Its origins are obscure but Margaret Gelling, one of the country's leading place-name scholars, has suggested the word means an 'ark' or 'chest'. The description suits the area around Winchcombe, lying in a valley bottom between surrounding hills. The area of Bishop's Cleeve lay near the heartland of the Hwiccan territory.

The details become clearer with the attempt to convert the people of Mercia to Christianity in the later seventh century. In 680 the bishopric of Worcester was established to minister to the Hwicce. The territory known as the parish of Bishop's Cleeve continued as part of this diocese until the foundation of the diocese of Gloucester at the Dissolution of the Monasteries nearly nine hundred years later. Within the former bishopric, minster churches were created from where a team of priests could evangelize the area. Minsters were built on royal estates where there was an existing population to convert. This is the clearest evidence we possess that people were living in the Bishop's Cleeve area. The estate belonged to the king, and it was consequently chosen as a site for a minster, dedicated to St Michael the Archangel, around the middle of the eighth century at the latest: at some time between 768 and 779, in order to support the minster, Offa, the famous king of Mercia, granted fifteen *mansiones*, or hides, of land at a place called *Timbingctun* lying adjacent to the estate already held by the minster *aet Clife*. The grant described the boundaries of the land, although unfortunately these now only survive in two eleventh-century copies, by which time the two areas had become one area assessed at thirty hides. This became the ancient ecclesiastical parish of Bishop's Cleeve, covering also Brockhampton, Gotherington, Southam, part of Stoke Orchard and

Woodmancote. It lasted as an important land unit for over a thousand years.

The life of the minster as an independent church was short. By 889 it had been taken over by the Bishop of Worcester. For the historian this was a fortunate development, for it ensured Bishop's Cleeve came into the hands of an institution which kept and preserved careful records. Without them our knowledge of Cleeve Hill and its common would be much the poorer.

The Land Charter

The charter now exists in two copies in the Cotton manuscripts in the British Museum. The earlier is known as Birch's *Cartularium Saxonicum* Number 246 and probably dates from the early eleventh century. A second copy was made later in the eleventh century at a difficult time for the church at Worcester for it had recently lost some of its manors — at Sodbury, Tetbury and Woodchester. This could explain some of the differences between the two copies. There was a careful redefining of the boundary on the eastern edge of the territory, where it might have been under threat of encroachment from the adjacent lands of Winchcombe Abbey. The lack of

This view of Southam illustrates how the *Timbingctun* estate was centred here rather than on Bishop's Cleeve, as Dr Grundy had supposed. The scarp remains heavily wooded even today

boundary clauses around Stoke Orchard at the western edge might suggest the land had already been lost to the church, as indicated in the Domesday Book when Bernard and Reginald were refusing to do service to Worcester for their part of the Cleeve estate.

The charters were first examined in print by Dr Grundy in 1935, and the introductory heading for this chapter is taken from his book. He suggested *Timbingctun* was the name of the land unit and Cleeve the name of the monastery. However, it is clear that the topographical description of

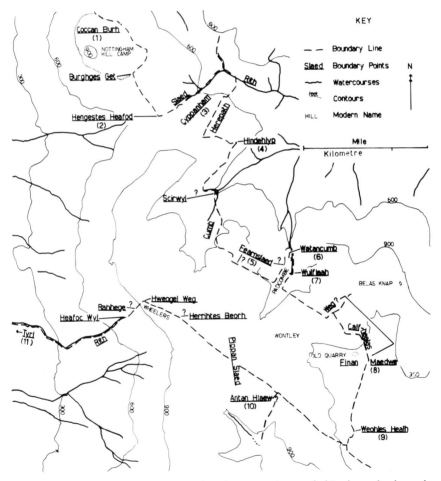

The boundary features defined in Birch's charter 246, recorded in the early eleventh century [Reproduced from the 1920 Ordnance Survey 6 in map with the permission of the Controller of Her Majesty's Stationery Office © Crown copyright]

Timbingctun, lying beneath *Wendlesclif* on the north side of the stream called *Tyrl*, accurately describes an estate within which the existing village of Southam now lies, and which could possibly have reflected the earlier territory discussed in the previous chapter. Evidence from other parts of the country, notably East Anglia, suggests that in this period settlements were mobile over short distances and that it is misleading to look for Anglo-Saxon settlements where there is one today. (Since Domesday, for example, a settlement probably lying between Southam and Stoke Orchard named *Sapletone* has completely disappeared.) By 991 the church at Worcester had created a new manor of two hides at Southam, and it seems reasonable to account for the loss of the name *Timbingctun* as the result of the merging of this estate with that of Cleeve, as recorded in the charter. The restructuring of the estate by 991 made the area subservient to Cleeve and therefore a new name reflected the new relationship – the manor of the southern settlement – Southam. This subservient relationship is still reflected in the Church of the Ascension at Southam which continues to be a chapel of ease associated with St Michael's in Bishop's Cleeve.

The complete bounds provide a fascinating glimpse into the landscape and economy of Bishop's Cleeve and its surrounding area during the late Saxon period, but here we are principally concerned with the evidence it provides for the development of the hill and the common. The whole area included a variety of land use to support the minster – arable, meadow, woodland and pasture. The careful definition of the boundaries around Cleeve Common indicate that it was now clearly attached to Bishop's Cleeve in the vale and that it had already become a crucial part of the local economy which the church at Worcester sought to defend against other claimants.

The Boundaries

Both charters have the boundary clauses in Old English, which has been used on the two maps on pages 24 and 29. The descriptions here in the text are in modern English, and to help identification, features which correspond in both descriptions have been given the same number. Birch's charter 246 can be translated as follows:

> From the gate of [Cocca's] camp (1) to Hengest's headland (2). So to the valley to Cyppa's enclosure (3) to a little stream. Along the little stream to the highway to hind's leap (4). Then to the clear spring. Along the combe to fern valley (5). Then to Pata's valley (6). Then to wolf clearing (7). Then to calf hollows along the way to woodpecker meadows (8), and so to wheel hollow (9), and so to Anta's barrow (10), and so to Pippa's valley and to Herriht's barrow, and to wheelway to the roedeer fence to the hawk spring along the small stream to the Tirle (11).

Looking out across Cyppa's enclosure to what is now Cockbury Butts in Prescott parish. The boundary follows the hedge cutting across the bottom of the photograph

The upland pastures of Cleeve Common and Postlip Warren are divided by this Cotswold stone wall. It is probable that it marks the line of the Saxon charter boundary but Postlip Warren was an area disputed between Cleeve and Winchcombe. It is recorded in Bishop's Cleeve parish on the 1841 Tithe Map [T.N. Curr]

The points correspond so closely with known points on the present parish boundary that a strong case can be made for the boundary having remained constant for over a thousand years until the present. Where there is some uncertainty the names have been given a question mark on the map. The details can easily be followed on any modern large scale Ordnance Survey map.

The camp is Nottingham Hill Iron Age hillfort. The parish boundary still defines Cyppa's enclosure to the north and north-east of Cockbury Court today, then follows the 'highway', between the stream and Cleeve Common, which was blocked up in 1823. Dr Grundy thought that at this point the boundary included Postlip Warren, but it seems more likely that, when standing at 'clear spring', it is the present boundary which runs 'along the combe' and excludes Postlip Warren. It then follows fern valley into Padcombe. The remaining name still surviving in the landscape is the 'wheel way' between points (10) and (11), where the boundary makes a sharp turn to the south-west above Queen's Wood to drop down suddenly off the plateau. In 1506 the field on the Prestbury side of the boundary was recorded as *Wheleways* and is still known as Wheeler's corner. Many other points can be identified with some certainty from the topography. They will be discussed in the next section.

Wheeler's corner, where the boundary makes a sudden turn off the high plateau above Southam. The photograph of the hillfort on page 12 provides an aerial view of the same place

As already noted the second copy defined very few landmarks in the western part of the territory but, fortuitously, it included much detail on the hill. The relevant part of the boundary is as follows:

From Cocca's camp (1) to Hengest's headland (2) to Cyppa's enclosure (3) to Tocca's camp (here the scribe seems to have made an error and copied again the first landmark) to hind's leap (4) to mill spring to clear spring to fern valley (5) to four ways to Pata's valley (6) where stand an apple tree and a maple tree which have grown together. From the trees to wolf clearing (7) to the old ditch to the Welsh way to limestone hill to woodpecker's meadow (8) to wheelway (9) to Sprog's clearing to the old ditch to the single thorn tree to Honta's barrow (10) to the steep wooded slope with a spring in it (*Swelhongre*) to the grey (or boundary) stone to the South Tirle (11).

As noted earlier, the church at Worcester seemed concerned to lay down a detailed description of the eastern boundary. The main reason probably lay in the interest in valuable pasture by communities lacking such grazing. Charlton Abbots, Sevenhampton and Prestbury all abut Cleeve common around its south eastern extremity along West Down. Much of the Cleeve boundary also forsakes natural features and cuts across the landscape in straight lines – clear topographical evidence of an artificial division. This is reinforced by boundary references to two 'old ditches'. From clearance in the Bronze Age to the present time, Cleeve has been able to dominate this area of downland despite pressure from neighbouring communities and landlords – although this is now difficult to trace solely from the landscape. For example, Sevenhampton's share of West Down was converted to arable after its enclosure in 1814. However the names West Down and West Wood do remain to suggest conflicting claims to the land on this part of the hill. The boundary cut West Wood into two and the Cleeve part was known as Wontley Wood. In 1833 it was cleared, leaving today's straight line running very close to the Saxon boundary. The wood and the down lie *east* of Cleeve. They are *west* of Winchcombe Abbey's territory. At what time and how any claims were reconciled in favour of Cleeve is not known, but it might not have been much earlier than the recording of these boundary clauses that Cleeve gained exclusive rights over land which had been open pasture for thousands of years and intercommoned by a number of communities. This provides further evidence for the conflict over possession of valuable resources of woodland and pasture on this part of the hill.

Work done on other charters suggests that estates were granted as working units and there is evidence – in the first charter, in the clauses defining the boundary on the vale – that the boundary there was considerably older than the recording, as there are three references to old (boundary) ditches. If the boundary here was defined as the population, and thus the pressure on the land, increased in the prehistoric period, then this part of the estate could have been nearly a thousand years old by the late eighth century. However, as discussed in Chapter One, on the hill the boundary might only have been formalized when the land grant made it necessary to put it in writing, either originally in the mid-eighth century or even shortly before the early eleventh century. The situation of an undivided upland pasture being shared by closely defined lowland territories has many

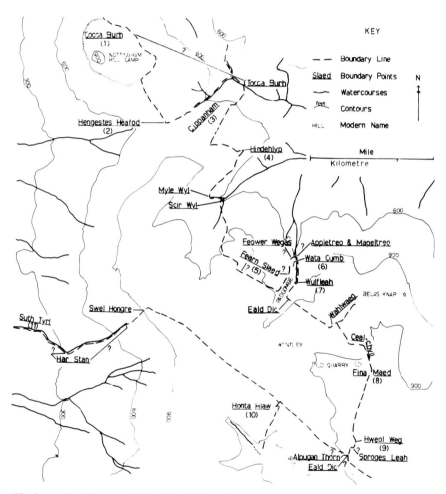

The boundary features defined in the late eleventh-century copy of the *Timbingctun* charter [Reproduced from the 1920 Ordnance Survey 6 in map with the permission of the Controller of Her Majesty's Stationery Office © Crown copyright]

The artificially straight western edge of West Wood reflects clearance on the Bishop's Cleeve side in 1833. The boundary actually runs through the field towards the building at the far side

parallels at this time, such as the Dartmoor example quoted in the Introduction.

Having now defined the extremities of the common and having established that it continued to be an area under pressure of differing claims, what can the bounds tell us about the landscape on Cleeve Hill in the Saxon period?

The Saxon Landscape

The estate was assessed at thirty hides in Domesday Book; this meant that by 1086 it paid tax at thirty units of assessment, but in the eighth century this would have meant literally that it could have supported thirty families. Two estate names, Cleeve and *Timbingctun*, have already been encountered, as have some personal names – Cocca, Cyppa, Pata – although whether these were legendary or real we do not know.

Pressure on the landscape pushed arable farming high up the scarp. Hengest's (a mythical name) headland, where the oxen were turned, reached

The importance of water supply for animals on the upland is reinforced by references in the boundary clauses. 'Hawk Spring' continues to provide water for cattle grazing on the upper slopes above Southam

up to Wickfield Lane near the route of the B4632; the parcel of land later farmed as Stony Cockbury estate was already in existence as Cyppas's enclosure; and at the end of West Down Sprog had made a clearing. There is ample evidence for the use of the downs as pasture for grazing of domestic and wild animals. Hindleap above Postlip, and Roedeer Fence above Southam probably indicated one-way jumps for wild animals on to the common, which protected nearby arable crops and provided for their easy capture. Water supply was a major problem for the stock and was probably the reason for the extension of the estate at the north end of Padcombe to incorporate the springs here. Wolf clearing reminds us of the dangers of keeping stock on the downs and also indicates the presence of some woodland at the far edge of the territory.

Woodland was another important resource in the local economy, providing timber for buildings and large items, coppiced wood for smaller items such as hurdles and handles, brushwood for lighting, and pannage for pigs. Wild bees provided honey and the woodland birds were killed for game. That part of West Wood lying in Cleeve, called variously East or Wontley Wood, grew timber. It is known only by implication from the boundary descriptions, lying next to woodpecker meadow, itself a valuable resource for winter hay and possibly corresponding to the two acres of meadow recorded in the Charlton Abbots entry in Domesday Book. Woodland on the slopes of the scarp, probably coppiced wood, was indicated by *Swel Hongre* above Southam in the later version. Later medieval clearance of such woodland had not yet taken place, and large areas of woodland must

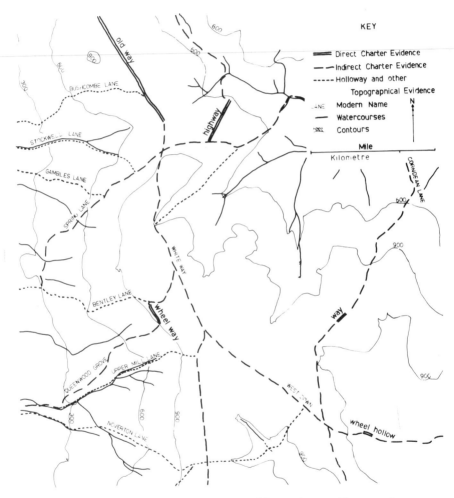

Cleeve Common and its scarp are criss-crossed by trackways. These are known to have been in existence by the early eleventh century; many are probably prehistoric (see Chapter One) [Reproduced from the 1920 Ordnance Survey 6 in map with the permission of the Controller of Her Majesty's Stationery Office © Crown copyright]

have extended across the face of Cleeve Hill despite ancient clearance in places. Today solitary thorn trees still grow at the far end of West Down, as recorded in the second copy of the boundaries.

The wider economy is also indicated in the boundary landmarks. The mill spring above Postlip (which on topographical evidence must correspond to the clear spring in the earlier charter) recorded in the later eleventh century is clear evidence for at least one mill at Postlip and suggests it was built after the first copy of the charter boundaries was drawn up. The reference to *Wendlesclif* in the introduction to the earlier charter provides evidence for quarrying at Cleeve Cloud. We do not know whether it had been actively exploited since the Romano-British period, for most buildings at this time were timber-built (probably including the minster church in Bishop's Cleeve). Quarrying was also suggested by the description of 'limestone hill' near Wontley.

Cleeve Common was not only an important local resource but also an area crossed by many trackways. Charter references to them have been marked on the two maps. They must predate the boundary as it used them as identifiable landmarks. Granna Lane, described in Chapter One, was referred to as Women's Way leading through Cockbury Camp and on to the common to fork and be picked up again in its eastern arm as wheel hollow, or way, leading from West Down and on to the Cotswolds through Roel

The remains of Wontley Farm showing clearly the 'Welsh Way' running south towards Wycomb

The holloway above Queenwood Grove, Prestbury, recommended by John Ogilby in 1675 as the main route between Gloucester and Coventry

Gate. The name Welsh Way, given to the track that runs north-east to south through the remains of Wontley farm, indicated a long distance trackway used by strangers or foreigners. Its route from Wycomb to Winchcombe can still be traced on the present large scale Ordnance Survey map. Another track crossed the hill, coming up from Prestbury as a holloway past Queenwood settlement, and recorded as *Wheleway* (now Wheeler's). It was by this track that John Ogilby recommended travellers between Gloucester and Coventry to cross the hill as late as 1675. From the hill it descended to Postlip along Dry Bottom; this is discussed further in Chapter Three. 'Four ways', recorded in the later copy of the boundaries, remains enigmatic. It was placed at the northern end of Padcombe yet there is little topographical or other documentary evidence to indicate a crossroads; this was perhaps another copying error.

This discussion of the trackways across the hill, many of them originating in prehistory is a convenient place to consider the mysterious stone block known as Huddlestone's Table which lies between the hamlet of Nutters-wood and the trees known as the Three Sisters (now only two remain). Many local folk-tales are told about it. By tradition it is said to mark one of the rare occasions when Cleeve Hill featured in what might loosely be called

Huddlestone's Table and the Three Sisters [T.N. Curr]

national history. The legend recounts that when Kenulf, king of Mercia, dedicated the great Benedictine Abbey in Winchcombe in 811, he took leave of several of his important guests at this spot, notable among them the king of Kent. However the evidence does not support this story.

Firstly, the parting would not have taken place at this spot. Not only has the stone been moved at various times in living memory, but the present spot is not on any trackway known to have been in use in 811 according to the charter and topographical evidence. Secondly, the parting could not have taken place at this stone, for the Huddleston family did not move to Southam until the 1520s, and even tradition accepts that they fashioned a replacement.

Nevertheless the stone has continued to intrigue observers. In 1779 the *Gentleman's Magazine* featured it in a short article which is more informative to the historian on eighteenth-century belief in Druids and mythology than about the stone itself. Likewise, the illustration taken from Emma Dent's *Annals of Winchcombe and Sudeley* informs us more about mid-Victorian Romanticism than about the stone. Both pieces, however,

Mr. URBAN,

I LaSt Summer met with Some traces of an irregular and not very extenSive encampment, upon the edge of the GlouceSterShire Hills, near Cleve-Clouds, and juSt above Cheltenham. Upon Some plain ground at a Small diStance below the edge of the hill, which on this Side forms a natural barrier to the encampment, is a large, nearly cubic, hewn Stone, with the following inScription upon its upper Surface:

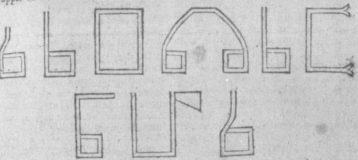

The characters Stand in the above order, Six in the firSt line, and three underneath; and are inScribed nearly in the middle of the upper Side of the Stone. On the Same Side, and Seemingly not long Since, has been cut with a tool, in Roman characters, HuddleSton's Table. Whether this is to be conSidered as the information of tradition, or of Some antiquarian who has inveStigated this piece of antiquity, is uncertain. All the information that was obtained at a village a Small diStance from hence, in the road to Cheltenham, relative to either the encampment or the Stone, was, that the trenches were thrown up in the time of Oliver Cromwell. But if the civil war in the laSt century had been more conSiderable and extenSive than it was, it could hardly have been the occaSion of more works of this kind than report now attributes to it in theSe parts of the kingdom, notwithStanding that, when the appeal was made to arms, the conteSt began, was chiefly continued, and terminated here. The Stone's being hewn into a regular figure, the uniformity of the characters, together with its Situation near an encampment, may be conSidered as Some proofs of the authenticity of this inScription.

As it is not noticed in Camden, and I have not been able to procure any information relative to it, Shall be much obliged by your inSertion of it, and to any gentleman that will favour me with his Sentiments upon it.

Yours, &c.   H. M. W.

BIOGRAPHICAL ANECDOTES, *from the* SUPPLEMENT *to* SWIFT.

Dr. FRANCIS HARE,

BRED at Eaton, was a Fellow of King's College, Cambridge, where he had the tuition of the Marquis of Blandford, only Son to the Duke of

againSt "The Conduct of the Allies." TheSe tracts, after being materially altered and amended by Mr. Maynwaring, were firSt publiShed under the inSpection of Mr. Oldmixon. Dr. Hare was alSo a writer in the Bangorian controverSy; and drew upon

The *Gentleman's Magazine* article on Huddlestone's Table in 1779 [Gloucester Library]

The origins of Huddlestone's Table – a mid-Victorian fantasy

illustrate the fascination with the unexplained, and although there is no evidence to link the stone to the story, if there ever was such a parting it could very well have taken place somewhere on the hill because of the network of trackways which crossed it.

The boundary clauses provide evidence of archaeological features which in some cases have subsequently been destroyed. Cocca's Camp exists as a feature in the landscape today and has given its name to an area immediately to the east of the camp where can be found Rushy Cockbury, Cockbury Butts and Stony Cockbury (now Cockbury Court), although only the latter lies in the parish of Bishop's Cleeve. Today Cockbury itself is known as Nottingham Hill, after William de Nottingham, who was the steward of the Bishop of Worcester between 1450 and 1470. Further round the bounds Anta's Barrow (wrongly identified as Belas Knap by Dr Grundy) and Herriht's Barrow lie on the long straight southern boundary of West Down, but are not readily identifiable today, although the former was still a feature when Samuel Rudder wrote his county history of 1779.

In this late Saxon period we know far more about the landscape and the boundary on the hill than about the people who exploited the landscape, and this, in turn, is a result of the change in the type of evidence from archaeological to documentary. The picture that has emerged of the hill from the land charter is of an area of upland plateau, extensively used for grazing by wild and domestic animals, essentially open as today except for a rather more wooded scarp. Even at this early date two recurring features are very apparent: one, people continuing to mould the landscape, with hindleaps, ditches, enclosures, clearings for arable, pasture and highways and, secondly, pressure on such a scarce resource which led to the detailed stating of the eastern limits in the late eleventh century. This pressure helps to explain the jagged route of the boundary of the present common. One major difference with today is that long-distance travellers moved across the pasture and not across the face of the scarp as does the present B4632. Essentially, however, the medieval manorial waste which became Cleeve Common would have been as recognizable to our Bronze Age ancestors as to ourselves today.

Domesday Book

The successful Norman takeover of 1066 would, like the Saxon takeover, seem to herald a new era in English history and provide an obvious starting point for the next chapter. Yet the great Domesday Book, which originated not very far away when William visited Gloucester for Christmas in 1085, should be seen rather as a statement of the nature of the countryside at the end of the Saxon period than an early description of the area in the later Middle Ages.

There is no record of how the local peasants viewed William's commissioners, but their answers are not particularly helpful in throwing additional light on the development of the hill in the later eleventh century. The Conquest itself had made little impact. Bishop Wulfstan continued as Bishop of Worcester but he was an absentee landlord; Bishop's Cleeve church was not rebuilt for almost another century, and no castle was ever built. Like most settlements in this area of Gloucestershire, the land belonging to the manor was overwhelmingly arable. The value of the manor had fallen from £36 immediately before the conquest to £26 in 1085. Presumably the bishop was having difficulty in administering his estate efficiently and Domesday carries evidence of the breakup of the estate. Bernard and Reginald held seven hides at Stoke and 'refused to do service to St Mary's', thus confirming the dispute over land which could be the reason for the omission of the western boundary of the estate in the second copy of its bounds. The territory of Bishop's Cleeve was recorded as the same thirty hides first recorded in the land charter, but by 1085 Gotherington, Southam and the now lost *Sapletone* had been leased by the bishop to Durand, the Sheriff of Gloucestershire who had been one of William's many followers rewarded by positions of authority and land grants after the victory at Hastings.

The subdivision of large estates is well documented as a feature of economic and social change in the late Saxon period and Cleeve fits into this pattern, illustrated by the development of the separate sub-manor of Southam in 991, when two hides were leased out by Bishop Oswald to Ethelstan his brother; by mid eleventh-century this sub-manor had increased to five hides; by Domesday it had expanded to six although its boundaries are not exactly known; in their final form they might have approximated to the later medieval manor, the boundaries of which were first recorded in 1472 (these are discussed more fully in the next chapter). Thus tenants of both Cleeve and Southam had rights to the hill and no doubt were already quarrelling over the assertion of those rights, as they were to continue to do so for nine hundred years. If we remember that the original land grant of the late eighth century referred to two separate areas of land which subsequently became one, it would seem that the thirty hide area entered in Domesday for Bishop's Cleeve only survived under the direct control of the Bishop of Worcester for less than two centuries. John Moore, the editor of the Phillimore edition of the Domesday Book for Gloucestershire, has identified a small manor granted to a riding man (who had to ride with messages for the bishop) worth one hide with land for two ploughs (about 240 acres) as the settlement at Wontley. Unfortunately, there is a lack of supporting evidence for this hypothesis.

Cleeve Hill lay on the edge of a great estate and it is fortunate that the Saxon charter copyists were so interested in defining the edges of landholding units, since this allows a clear understanding of a landscape not very different from that of today; rather more woodland, especially on the scarp; certainly more arable on the scarp; but mostly pasture for grazing, for this upland plateau was marginal not only to the forerunners of the communities at Bishop's Cleeve and Southam, but to those of the other communities which had claimed a part for themselves – Prestbury, Sevenhampton, Charlton Abbots and Winchcombe. Into this landscape we can begin to place personal names, if not real people – Cocca, Hengest, Cyppa, Pata, Sprog – and this implies that people were clearly responsible in their own small ways for developing the landscape. The hill was marginal to the settlements but it had already emerged as a scarce resource. As the quantity of topographical and documentary evidence increases, we can also begin to distinguish sub-themes within the competition for land use: between manors, between pasture for grazing, woodland, settlement, and recreation. It seems sensible to divide up the succeeding chapters into these sub-themes. The silent, majestic appearance of the hill today belies a cacophony of voices from the past each making their own claim.

FURTHER READING

This chapter has been based upon extensive fieldwalking following the boundaries of the two land charters printed in G.B. Grundy, *Saxon Charters and Fieldnames of Gloucestershire*, Volume 1 (Bristol and Gloucestershire Archaeological Society, Bristol, 1935) pages 71–90. The interpretations have been helped by careful study of the 6 in Ordnance Survey map of 1882. A.H. Smith, *The Place Names of Gloucestershire* (Cambridge University Press, Cambridge, 1965) has helped with the resolution of place-names, particularly in pages 86–95 in Volume 2. John Moore's translation and commentary upon Domesday, published as *Gloucestershire Domesday Book* (Phillimore, Chichester, 1982), has helped the discussion on Domesday.

Several books have helped with the wider context. Carolyn Heighway's *Anglo-Saxon Gloucestershire* (Alan Sutton Publishing, Gloucester, 1987) is a convenient summary of the period. Christopher Dyer's *Lords and Peasants in a Changing Society* (Cambridge University Press, Cambridge, 1981) and *Standards of Living in the Later Middle Ages* (Cambridge University Press, Cambridge, 1989) put the area into the context of the Bishop of Worcester's estates. Della Hooke's *The Anglo-Saxon Landscape* (Manchester University Press, Manchester, 1985) recreates the landscape of the Hwicce by exploiting the potential of the West Midland Saxon land charters for this purpose. Another view of the development of the territory of Hwicce is provided by Steven Bassett in a collection of essays edited by him as *The Origins of the Anglo-Saxon Kingdoms* (Leicester University Press, Leicester, 1989). Further discussion of boundaries appears in Chapter Eight of Margaret Gelling's book on place-names, *Signposts to the Past* (Dent, London, 1978). A more general approach can be found in her later book *Place-names in the Landscape* (Dent, London, 1984). The latest thinking on the nature of settlement in the period is discussed by Christopher Taylor in *Village and Farmstead* (George Philip and Son, London, 1983), which also has relevance, as do the books of Christopher Dyer, for the succeeding chapters.

CHAPTER THREE

Searching for Hidden Landscapes
(1086–c. 1520)

The Lord Bishop of Worcester is lord of the manor and patron of
the church.
Survey of Bishop's Cleeve 1299 in *Red Book of Worcester*, Vol. IV,
1950

Sources and Contexts

During the later Middle Ages a wealth of evidence for the use of Cleeve Hill
can be extracted from the records of the Bishop of Worcester, whose
carefully administered estates gave rise to much documentation, not only
for his manor of Bishop's Cleeve but also for his other manors scattered
around the West Midlands. These have been meticulously analysed by
Christopher Dyer in his book *Lords and Peasants in a Changing Society*,
which provides the wider context for the material investigated in this
chapter. The manorial court rolls for Cleeve, and especially the detailed
surveys of *c.* 1170 and 1299, form the backbone to this chapter and give the
opportunity to re-people the later medieval landscape and spy on the lives of
its creators and users – the luckless medieval peasants for whom life was
often hard and generally short.

The major development of this period for the historian is the increasing
quantity of documentary evidence to complement that of the landscape. The
first records of the upland pasture as common land come in *c.* 1150; the first
reference to stinting, in the thirteenth century; the first clear record of the
names of people living on the hill, in 1299; the first detailed records of
quarrying, from 1389; and by 1482 the first reference to a defined boundary
across the common separating Bishop's Cleeve manor from Southam
manor. We know much more about Bishop's Cleeve manor in the later
Middle Ages than we do about Southam because the former lay under the
direct control of the bishop, but the latter passed through the hands of
sub-tenants and very few records have survived. All the records confirm the
already established dominant theme of the hill's history – pressure on a

scarce resource and conflict over its use – but the written record allows the historian to chart more precisely the changes affecting the hill and its landscape.

Before looking at how the hill was used and moulded by the medieval peasant, it should be considered in the wider context of the manor under the Bishop of Worcester's jurisdiction. It is essential to appreciate that it was but one part of a far more extensive landholding held by the bishop, in order to understand its working as it appeared to contemporaries. Having an absentee landlord meant that Bishop's Cleeve and its people were always susceptible to outside influences. His manors stretched from Hartlebury and Alvechurch in the north to Westbury-on-Trym in the south; from Bredon and Fladbury in the vale to Blockley and Bibury on the high wold. No manor was totally self-sufficient and all were to some degree interdependent. Cleeve had over a thousand acres of upland grazing and in summer could support sheep from the lowland manors as well as its own, but by 1246 Cleeve was itself subservient to Blockley manor as the centre for sheep flocks before the clipping. In its turn Cleeve depended on other manors: most of its hay came from the fifty acres of meadow land by the River Avon at Bredon, still known as Cleeve Meadow; its pigs were pastured in the woods at Welland near Malvern; and lacking adequate supplies of timber, when the Bishop's great barn was built – or rebuilt – in 1465, the large timbers were brought down from Hartlebury. They still survive in what is now misleadingly called the Tithe Barn. The timber came down the Severn to Tewkesbury, which was a favourite transport route. In 1396/7 the rector of Bishop's Cleeve bought firewood from Alveley in Shropshire, where he had another living. Tewkesbury was an important market centre for Bishop's Cleeve, and we know the tenants also visited Gloucester and Winchcombe to trade. People continued to move around the landscape, as they have done at all periods.

During these centuries after Domesday the peasants of Cleeve who moulded the landscape lived in a world where they were subject to influences and controls from the wider world: influences which are in danger of being ignored in favour of a romantic vision of self-contained and self-sufficient local communities. This is the value of the documents as their increasing number enables a deeper understanding of the changes which can still be traced in the present landscape – if patient study allows the meaning of its hidden messages to be revealed.

Farming the Scarp

On the steep slopes of Cleeve between the western wall of the common at the top and Woodmancote at the bottom lies a lost landscape created by increasing numbers of peasants scratching a living from the thin shifting soil

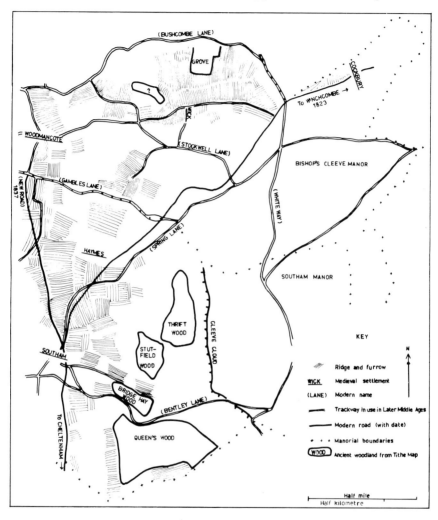

(BUSHCOMBE LANE)

GROVE

?

COCKBURY

To WINCHCOMBE
1823

WICK

WOODMANCOTE

(STOCKWELL LANE)

BISHOP'S CLEEVE MANOR

(GAMBLES LANE)

(NEW ROAD)
1837

(WHITE WAY)

(SPRING LANE)

HAYMES

SOUTHAM MANOR

THRIFT
WOOD

CLEEVE CLOUD

KEY

N

SOUTHAM

STUT-
FIELD
WOOD

BRIDGE
HAY

(BENTLEY LANE)

Ridge and furrow

WICK   Medieval settlement

(LANE)   Modern name

Trackway in use in Later Middle Ages

Modern road (with date)

Manorial boundaries

WOOD   Ancient woodland from Tithe Map

TO CHELTENHAM

QUEEN'S WOOD

Half mile

Half kilometre

The surviving medieval features referred to in this chapter

ever higher up the scarp, until the increased arable areas threatened the
equally valuable upland grazing of the common. Today, the best time to
view this landscape is in winter when the melting snow, or long contrasting
shadows cast by the low sun, pick out the ridge and furrow, the trackways
and deserted settlements of that period of medieval agricultural expansion.

Population growth probably halted in the second decade of the fourteenth century and contracted more rapidly after the Black Death of 1348–9. Although there is evidence that cultivation of these fields continued for at least another century, when the medieval ploughteam finally retreated to the more amenable lands in the vale, they left a pattern on the landscape which remains to this day.

The map on page 43 is an attempt to recreate this hidden landscape between Southam and Bushcombe Lane using the evidence of aerial photographs, field walking, eighteenth- and nineteenth-century maps and field names, particularly those taken from the 1841 Tithe Award. Bushcombe Lane is an arbitrary historical boundary but its choice enables us to include an area which is really a continuation of the Cleeve Hill landscape. It cannot be claimed that the map is faultless. In some places the evidence is difficult to interpret. In other places soil slumping has destroyed medieval features, and towards the top of the scarp the construction of the present B4632 in 1823 led to the destruction of medieval features long before the modern requirement to record what was being destroyed. However, the main outline is quite clear. It is dominated by the corrugated, slightly curving ridge and furrow typical of medieval arable cultivation. The current explanation is that it was created by the simple medieval plough with its fixed mould board which cast the soil always to the same side, so that the soil was gradually moved towards the centre of each ridge from the edge. Most of the ridges run with the slope, to improve drainage, and consequently the ploughing also led to a certain amount of soil creep which accounts for changes in levels either side of field boundaries, upslope being higher and downslope often much lower. Such a problem is not, of course, particular to Cleeve, for the whole of the Cotswold scarp from Bath to Chipping Campden is covered with similar cord-like sinews gathered together into blocks or furlongs. Where such areas of land were added to existing areas they are known as 'assarts'. They reflect the work of the medieval ploughman desperate to increase cultivated land because of growing population and the low yields from the seed. Christopher Dyer has calculated that c. 1300 returns of the main crops of wheat and barley were fourfold in a good year and under threefold in a poor year. Expansion of arable land suggests population growth. The written records confirm this.

Domesday Book of 1086 records forty-five people in the area, eight of whom were slaves without a claim to the land. The survey of c. 1170 listed eighty-three tenants, and one taken in 1299 contained 102 names. We can assume that generally each recorded tenant represented one family but we know nothing of the unrecorded sub-tenants beyond that they existed – but it may be assumed that their numbers grew at least in the same proportions. There is an indication from the evidence that this increase in population led to a halving in the size of the average family holding from sixty acres in 1086 to thirty acres in 1299, and this in turn prompted demands to bring more land under the plough. The process of assarting is most clearly seen in the survey of Bishop's Cleeve, Woodmancote and Wontley taken in *c.* 1170. Assarted land is recorded as follows: in Woodmancote Robert Franceys 1 yardland (about 30 acres), John and Engelbalt 3 acres, Edric and Sefare 9 acres, and Gladwyn 4 acres; in Cleeve, Samson the priest (who had his own small manor separate from the bishop's manor) 3 acres, and Girold 185 acres; in Wontley 'a certain new land' paying 8d. All assarts, except Girold's, but including the larger assarts of Robert Franceys, were but a small proportion of the tenants' total holdings, suggesting perhaps, piecemeal enclosing of small areas of land at the margin of their existing holding. It is impossible to identify these small assarts today – although they may be the explanation for the small irregular shape of many of the fields on the hill slopes. Here the ridge and furrow stops at the field boundary indicating the field was reclaimed from pasture or woodland before being ploughed. Contrast this with the longer established arable land of the vale where the modern field boundaries tend to run in straight lines, ignoring the underlying ridge and furrow which were a result of enclosure largely of the eighteenth and nineteenth centuries. Here the ridge and furrow came before the enclosing field boundaries.

Between Gambles Lane and Stockwell Lane the melting snow picks out the ridge and furrow running up to an earlier track. In the distance the ridge and furrow on what is possibly Girold's assart can also be distinguished

The one notable exception to this small scale development is the assarting of a tenant who is known to us only as Girold. Both Professor Finberg and Christopher Dyer have studied this shadowy figure and have been able to draw some general conclusions about the nature of assarting. It is a tale worth repeating here. The entry in the survey reads:

> Girold in Cleeve [holds] twelve acres which used to pay 3s. and another assart of four acres which paid 12d., and three acres which were Godfrey's which paid 4d., and four acres which were Richard's for 8d., and in addition to this one hundred and forty three and a half acres of assart with wood which remains to be assarted. The total of Girold's assart is one hundred and seventy acres. And it is half in one field and half in the other, and for it he pays one mark, [13s. 4d.] by [grant of] Bishop Roger and in addition to this he holds fifteen acres of assart for 3s.

It seems likely that Girold started off with the original twelve acres paying 3s. each year but then added to his holding by both acquisition and assarting until he reclaimed a huge assart of $143\frac{1}{2}$ acres from wood or pasture land. A possible location for Girold's assart is the vast area of spindly ridge and furrow now reverted to low quality scrub pasture beneath Longwood Common and dropping down to the fold between Nottingham and Cleeve Hills above the small medieval settlement of Wick.

The example of Girold can be further used to illustrate features of assarting which survive so clearly on the scarp today. His original holding was valued at 4d. per acre; some of the smaller assarts, presumably on better arable land, also paid a similar sum. The one hundred acres, however, paid only 1d. per acre rent – a clear sign that the poorer quality land on the hill slopes was now being cultivated as a result of population pressure. Bishop Roger acquiesced in this assarting because he was grateful for any increase in his annual income from his manor, at that time worth 100s. 8d. in total.

Girold was the first peasant on record who seemed to have control over labour and capital independent of his lord, Bishop Roger. He was the known precedent for a type of peasant who became increasingly typical of the population in Bishop's Cleeve in contrast to the greater hold by their landlords over the villagers of Southam. However, even in Bishop's Cleeve Girold did not possess complete freedom to use his assart as he liked. The clause 'And it is half in one field and half in the other' is a reminder of the byelaws and traditions concerning cropping and fallowing, dates of ploughing, harvesting and opening of the stubble to grazing, the observation of which was integral to community well being and cooperation. It also points to the inadequacies of relying solely on the landscape itself as evidence for its own past.

The c. 1170 survey probably recorded the greatest period of assarting, for in the other great survey, that of 1299, there are almost no references to it. This is unsurprising if it can be accepted that the number of tenants – which grew from forty-five to eighty-three between Domesday and *c.* 1170 – rose to only 102 by 1299. The number of sub-tenants is unknown; in the mid-thirteenth century one tenant had twenty-one sub-tenants! This figure may not be typical, but it gives heightened evidence for the effects of population pressure on the land. Assuming, however, that their change in numbers parallelled that of the recorded tenants, increasing demands on land were slackening. Perhaps it was as a consequence of this that the 1299 survey recorded only two pieces of land still identifiable to contemporaries as assarts. Gregory de Marerny, a free tenant, held half a yardland and one assart for 5s. 10d. The usual rent for half a yardland was 4s. so the assart could have been worth 1s. 10d., and was likely therefore to have been between ten and fifteen acres, allowing for inflation during the thirteenth century. Walter ate Wyke, living in Wick, held a cotland of fifteen acres for 3s., a furlong for 14d., a grove for 3s. and an assart for 18d. The grove could either have been the area marked 'grove' on the Tithe Map (see page 43), in which faint traces of ridge and furrow can still be seen, or the present coppice woodland above The Roundhouse, with either the furlong or the assart being the crescent-shaped piece of land immediately above it – the

Evidence of the land hunger of the later Middle Ages can be glimpsed in this winter view of the ridge and furrow above Woodmancote

cramped position of which highlights the land hunger of the later Middle Ages. A third reference, twenty-nine and a half acres of *frisce* (land ploughed occasionally), probably relates to land on the scarp but its location has never been identified.

By 1299 assarting was coming to an end and the hidden landscape which can be detected on the scarp today represents the maximum extent of arable land use by the first decade of the fourteenth century. This happened for a variety of reasons, of which fall in population is the most obvious. There were crops of barley and wheat, with the odd patch of oats growing high up the hillside. The soils were thin but the west and south-west aspects were favourable enough for vines to grow on Bushcombe.

The numbers of tenants on the bishop's manor of Cleeve fell by 35 per cent between 1299 and 1349, mostly as a result of the Black Death, and although tithe records show that ploughed land did not decrease by the same proportion, the population decline obviously took pressure off the upland slopes. Apart from occasional use for crops in the succeeding centuries, they have remained as pasture, thus presenting a clear impression of the medieval landscape at its greatest extent.

This spread of arable land up the scarp contrasted with the latter's other value to the manor, for more arable meant less pasture and woodland, both essential to the manorial economy and, with the exception of the common, remarkably scarce on this manor. An indication of their importance is provided in the survey of 1299, when the value of pasture on Bushcombe, which had undoubtedly been eaten into by assarting, stood at 20s. per annum; value of the underwood (indicating that Bushcombe Wood was then, as today, coppiced woodland) stood at 5s.; and pannage for pigs in the wood was valued at 12d. The straight lines of the present south-east boundary of the wood are clear indications that the wood had been cut back to provide animal pasture. It might have been the wood 'which remains to be assarted' on Girold's holding in *c.* 1170. The best evidence for opposition to this late thirteenth-century decline of pasture is recorded for another of the bishop's manors, notably on heaths north of Alvechurch, where enclosures were thrown down by the men of King's Norton at some time before 1273. In Bishop's Cleeve in 1462 John Sewell was ordered to remove a fence he had used to make a private enclosure on the common at Kerr's Hill on Bushcombe, probably land lying to the south of Bushcombe Lane at its steepest part – a reminder that open land bordering the roadways was also regarded as common.

Assarting took place in many areas of marginal land during the later Middle Ages, not only here and along the whole Cotswold scarp but also on the bishop's other manors. The *c.* 1170 survey recorded five acres at Gotherington; the *Landboc* of Winchcombe Abbey recorded arable land at Padcombe and Langley on high, sloping ground just over Cleeve Hill in *c.* 1317; and Christopher Dyer has estimated that over two thousand acres were added to the arable land of the Bishop of Worcester's manors at this time which, although a small proportion of the total of thirty of forty thousand acres, could be locally of greater significance, as here on the slopes of Cleeve and Nottingham Hills.

The scarp is a major source of reference because so much of the field evidence remains visible today, and it can allow a fuller interpretation of the pattern of fields and paths on the slopes of Cleeve Hill. However, arable expansion was not the only change to affect the later medieval landscape of the hill; woodland too underwent changes during this period.

Woodland

The reference to Bushcombe Wood indicates that woodland was an important resource of the manor. Coppiced woodland was cut about every seven years to provide wood for furniture, tool handles, wattles, fences and hurdles. In 1302/3 and 1389/90 there are references to the cutting of hawthorn in Bushcombe Wood for the making of dead hedges and enclosures. Pannage for pigs in Bushcombe Wood was valued at 12d. in 1299. Honey from wild bees and game also provided the villagers with further valuable resources. Timber came from high woodland, notably from Wontley and from trees scattered around the landscape. Much of the

A further view of the presumed area of Girold's assart with Bushcombe Wood on the skyline at the top of the Nottingham Hill scarp

This view out of Queen's Wood confirms its existence in the later Middle Ages. The ridge and furrow respects its boundary, and constant ploughing down the slope has lowered the surface of the field

evidence available from immediately after Domesday is indirect and fragmentary, although Domesday noted 'a little wood' (either Bushcombe Wood or Wontley Wood). The place-name Woodmancote (woodman's cottage) which was first recorded in the *c.* 1170 survey, is perhaps an indication of woodland clearance, but archaeologists and historians agree place-names are difficult to interpret. The continuing existence of woodland at this time, however, is evidenced by reference to a swineherd and two woodwards, or wood keepers, in that survey. By 1299 more evidence appears and survives, and apart from a major clearance of Wontley Wood in the early nineteenth century, the present pattern of woodland seems to have been established by this time, with Wontley Wood used for growing timber; the woodland on the scarp slopes of Nottingham Hill, by now only those areas unsuited for arable or pasture, being used as coppiced woodland; and the areas of woodland including the present Queen's, Thrift and Stutfield Woods being a mixture of timber trees, pollards and coppiced woodland. The reeve of the manor of the rector of Bishop's Cleeve took a wainload of wattles from these woods in 1391/2. In many places the medieval boundary bank still survives, indicating the stable nature of the boundaries at least by the end of this period.

The wood at Wontley was a scarce resource of standing timber, so it is not surprising that both the Bishop of Worcester, and the Abbot of Winchcombe, who shared it, went to great lengths to protect its value and the use of its trees. The two woodwards recorded in 1299 lived at Wontley. The wood was valued at £40 in *c.* 1440, when the underwood was valued at 13s. 4d., a figure unchanged since 1299. In 1474/5 the bishop's bailiff was paid a quarter of wheat per annum for keeping the wood, and in 1505/6 the wood was fenced to keep out animals as the land which had been farmed around Wontley was then let for grazing. The importance of the timber to Winchcombe can be measured from a plea from the burgesses to Mary Tudor some time between 1553 and 1558. She had replaced the abbot as landlord and they pleaded to her not to grant the wood away, for its seventy acres provided the only timber good enough to repair the Queen's estimated eighty to a hundred houses and five mills in Winchcombe, because the other two woods on the manor, Deepwood and Humleyhoo, were described as coppiced woodland. This is a further indication that the problems of management of scarce resources were not peculiar to Cleeve in this, or any other period.

The Common as Grazing Ground

It is the increasing documentation regarding the use of the common that reveals the conflicts created by demands on its natural resources – conflicts which have left some record in the landscape but which are closely identifiable only from the written record. These demands in this later medieval period were those of sheep grazing, or overgrazing, and quarrying.

In *c.* 1150 William de Solers established a chapel at Postlip and granted to the priest a house, half a yardland and common rights for six cattle and one horse with his other domesticated animals, on the common pasture above Postlip. By inference we have here the earliest known written reference to the common pasture. The reference could indicate continuation of intercommoning; it could also suggest that what is now Postlip Warren still lay outside the Cleeve territory, as discussed previously. The grant attempted to lay down the number of animals the priest could put on the common pasture relative to the size of his holding, and gives an early example of stinting.

Professor W.G. Hoskins has shown how references to stinting became more frequent as manorial court records become more numerous throughout southern lowland England from the thirteenth century. At the same time a growing population increased the need for animals, especially to keep arable land fertile. This was recognized by parliament, which passed the Statute of Merton in 1236 forbidding lords to enclose common pastures unless they left adequate common for the freeholders. The problem of overgrazing was particularly acute from March to June every year, when both winter and spring sown crops were growing on the arable land and the meadow was closed to grazing before the hay harvest. Animals could graze only on the fallow field. This heightened the importance of the common pasture on the hill plus a small acreage at Longwood Common on Nottingham Hill. There was little other permanent pasture, only enough to support forty oxen or cows in 1299.

Stinting was first recorded in Bishop's Cleeve during the thirteenth century, when a freeholding of at least twenty acres provided grazing rights for two oxen, a cow and calf. However, frequent references to byelaws in the court rolls attempting to control stinting after 1400 suggest the stints were unenforceable, although overgrazing for the individual's profit was clearly seen as detrimental to the community. The problems increased after 1470 when the bishop no longer had his own sheep flock, as part of his movement out of direct management of his own lands, and his tenants took advantage of the increased potential for grazing on the common. By 1538 a peasant yardland brought the right to stint thirty sheep on the common. It seems that by 1400 at the latest the typical flock was the small peasant one, but added together they produced enormous numbers of animals grazing on Cleeve Common. If, as can be estimated, about fifty people with such rights lived in Bishop's Cleeve at that date, even if the stint was obeyed, 1,500 sheep could be put to graze on Cleeve Common, in addition to unknown numbers belonging to Southam tenants who were, of course, no longer under the direct control of the Bishop of Worcester. The problem of overgrazing must have been worse in 1299 because we know that the bishop himself had kept one thousand sheep on the hill in summer and two hundred in winter, moving most off to winter in his vale manors. The pasture for each hundred was valued as 12d. The total number of the peasants' flocks is unknown, but at the end of the fourteenth century, the rector's tithes of newborn lambs indicated a combined total of tenants' flocks in the whole of the parish (Bishop's Cleeve and Southam manors) of between three and four thousand. To this we must add the bishop's own flock, recorded as 360 wethers on 29 September 1389 – a date by which the ewes and lambs had already moved off the manor. This is the only source for the later Middle Ages which allows an estimate of the total number of sheep likely to have been on the hill at any one time. This was probably around five thousand, which represents five sheep per acre of common without taking into account sheep from the rector's own manor nor the cattle or horses, also grazing the common.

Despite the importance of sheep to the manor, after 1246 Bishop's Cleeve became subservient to Blockley as the hub of the bishop's sheep farming business. There the sheep were driven for shearing or, if they had been clipped in Cleeve, just their wool was sent. A reference in 1450 to Helena Wollemonger, and a house called 'Wollemongers', gives some evidence that then, or in the previous generation or so, the peasants of Bishop's Cleeve could have been taking some control over the selling of the woolclip from their own sheep.

The written records offer information on the scale of sheep farming in Bishop's Cleeve in the later Middle Ages, but there are few clues to be found in the landscape, because the profits were taken out of the area; it is in the wool towns such as Chipping Campden and Northleach that are found the churches associated with the wealth of the wool trade. One contemporary feature in the landscape gives an indication of the pressure brought upon land: the division of the common into parcels of Bishop's Cleeve and Southam manors. In the absence of direct evidence it must be assumed that there was intercommoning on the hill between the tenants of Cleeve manor and the tenants of the two parts of the manor of Southam which the bishop had granted out, initially in 991 as a two hide manor. However, with the enclosure of the lands of the deserted settlement at Wontley by 1482, and consequent lack of intercommunal grazing there, the pressure created by the demand for grazing led to the restating of a boundary which can still be traced by boundary stones lined across the common and marked on large scale Ordnance Survey maps.

The earliest recording lies in a document in the Public Record Office in London, and is concerned with a dispute of 1563 which is discussed in Chapter Four. However, the description quoted here is from a slightly later but much more detailed definition occurring in a similar document for 1591, in which reference is made to its existence in the same form in 1482:

> . . . and so to a way call *Smale Way* which divides this manor [i.e. Stoke Orchard] and the manor of Cleeve, following the same way eastward as it leads to *Birkmore* to the Cross Way there, And there hence eastward as *steare waie* leads to *Chappmandeane* and so forward to *potteslipp* quarry, from there east and south to *hore* stone to the north corner of *Wontloe* pasture, and so following the east hedge thereof southwards as it leads to *Wontloe* south corner, therehence returning westward as *heath hedge* leads to certain stumps or hillocks towards *Whelewaies* corner and so by the utter southmost hedge of *Queene Woode* to *Keane lease* corner . . .'

This boundary has been marked on the map on page 54. It can be followed with certainty by the boundary stones, except where they diverge for some unknown reason from the *steare waie* and take a more easterly course for a short distance. We do not know how many boundary stones there were

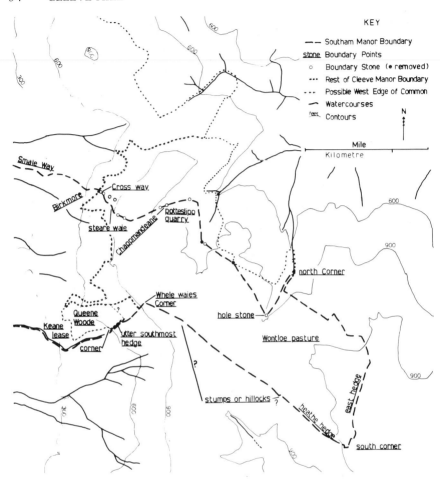

The boundary of Southam manor as recorded in a court case of 1591, in which the inclusion of Wontley was a claim. In reality the boundary would have run generally southwards from 'hole stone' to the northern edge of West Down (see page 62) [Reproduced from the 1920 Ordnance Survey 6 in map with the permission of the Controller of Her Majesty's Stationery Office © Crown copyright]

originally across the common, for in 1882, when the Ordnance Survey commissioners surveyed the boundaries of the parish for inclusion on their large-scale maps, they noted that two stones were known to have been removed. Three identical stones now stand in a field lower down the hill off Ashleigh Lane, presumably their new home by 1882.

The best preserved boundary stone is undoubtedly the third stone on the common near the King's Beeches. The present stones date possibly from the early nineteenth century [T.N. Curr]

This boundary definition may have reflected the prehistoric territories discussed in Chapter One, particularly in its use of the linear ditch across the common. However, the growth of Southam manor from two hides in 991 to six hides by Domesday might indicate the area was not the same. The reference to Wontley lying within Southam manor is puzzling: until 1623 it was part of Bishop's Cleeve manor. The best possible explanation for this claim can be found in the nature of the document. It formed part of a court case in which Southam tenants were arguing their lack of grazing on Cleeve Common as a result of the common being shared between Bishop's Cleeve and Southam manors. Both had presumably previously enjoyed rights of intercommoning at Wontley between its fourteenth-century desertion and its enclosure in 1482, and the best way, they felt, to have those rights restored was to claim Wontley lay in Southam manor. This pretence had the desired effect in law, but not in practice (see Chapter Four).

At the end of the Middle Ages *Smale* (or 'narrow') way ran up the hill and is known as Gambles Lane today; Birkmore is now Bittemoor and its

This example marks 'hole stone'. It has slumped over but the reversed S for Southam can still be clearly seen. Most of the other remaining stones are split and illegible

recording here evidences that certainly by 1591 (and possibly by 1482) this area of rough grazing was no longer common land, even if it had once been so. Cross Way is where Spring Lane meets Rising Sun Lane and was the track which became turnpiked in 1797 as the Cheltenham to Evesham road via Winchcombe. The *staere waie* is best seen from the vale as a very striking line cutting diagonally across the scarp, looking exactly like a staircase; the view from the common is too close to appreciate the aptness of the description. The earlier definition of 1563 describes the linear ditch running across the side of an area called *Wylbyngton* – a name now lost – before also describing Dry Bottom as *Chappmandeane*, i.e., 'the valley of the travelling merchant'. This gives clear evidence that the route across the common from *Whelewaies* corner to Postlip, identified from the Saxon charter, was still in use as a long distance routeway in the late sixteenth century.

Potteslipp quarry helps up to identify the actual quarry rented out by the Bishop of Worcester to the Abbot of Winchcombe in this period. From there the boundary runs almost straight to *hore* ('grey') stone where one of the boundary stones still stands. Here it meets the parish boundary north of

Wontley which it was then described as following around the former fields of Wontley and all the way back to the vale. Although the rights to the area enclosed by the boundary could be a cause for dispute, the topographical details were not. Three points on this final part are of significance, the most obvious being the recording again of *Whelewaies* as a boundary feature. There is the reference to 'stumps or hillocks', one of which must be the *Wontloe* or Wontley barrow. This must have been the *Hunta hlawe* of the Saxon charter bounds, not Belas Knap as identified by Dr Grundy in 1935, which has misled scholars ever since. The features referred to here are difficult to trace today but could be the reason for the humps near the entrance to the common by the radio masts. Finally, and perhaps most surprisingly, the long West Down boundary was marked by a hedge, not a wall. The traditional Cotswold drystone wall, considered so much an unchanged part of the landscape, seems to have appeared here only in the early years of the nineteenth century. Maps of other Cotswold estates generally support this observation that the Cotswold stone field wall, stretching out across the wolds, is a relatively recent feature appearing ubiquitously only since *c.* 1800. The medieval Cotswold landscape was largely open field arable and would have appeared little different from the landscape in the vale. Even the peasants' houses were timber-framed. The 'traditional' Cotswold landscape is of very recent origin.

The need to define the boundary was the result of increasing pressure on the common when its perimeter boundaries had been more or less defined and any change in the boundary was the result of encroachment, not expansion. The boundary defined the grazing areas for the animals of the tenants of Cleeve and Southam manors, and the continuing conflict between the two sets of tenants is clearly documented in the post-medieval period, discussed in Chapter Four. However the need to define the boundary was also important in controlling quarrying, which was now increasingly documented and which, of course, not only destroyed animal pasture but also created hazards for the animals. The lord held the right to quarry the stone, and by leasing out this right a small income could be made. It was therefore important to know who possessed such rights over which parts of the common.

Quarrying

The two areas of quarrying which are recorded in the Bishop of Worcester's records are at Postlip and Cleeve Cloud. These have always been the best recorded. Direct references to the processes of quarrying do not exist. Postlip Quarry was rented for 6d. per annum to the Abbot of Winchcombe from at least 1393 to the Dissolution in 1540. The court rolls tell us no more than that. Presumably the abbot used the stone principally for the abbey

Postlip Quarry was rented to the Abbot of Winchcombe throughout the Middle Ages. Worked extensively in the eighteenth and nineteenth centuries, it was one of the last to be worked in this century [T.N. Curr]

building, and to provide stone for the building of Winchcombe church at the end of the fifteenth century as a joint venture between himself, the townspeople and Ralph Boteler of Sudeley. We can, however, glean from the record that the quarries were worked when required rather than continuously as a source of profit. Stone sold from a quarry at *Weryngewell*, now unidentifiable, was worth 9d. to the bishop in 1425/6 but nothing in the following year because nobody would rent it. We have references in 1392 and 1394 and 1426/7 that the quarry at Cleeve Cloud was occupied by a tenant who refused to pay rent; another indication that in this period the bishop's direct influence in his manor was lessening. The quarries were probably seen by the bishop as a source of building stone for his needs rather than a source of profit through leasing to others. Stone was needed for his manor house in Bishop's Cleeve, and for the building and upkeep of Cleeve church. In 1389/90 five hundred slates for the chancel of Bishop's

Although documentary evidence does not survive until the sixteenth century, these houses in Gambles Lane reflect a pattern of roadside encroachments by squatters in the Middle Ages

Cleeve church cost 15d. and the carting of them from Ash Quarry (possibly near Cleeve Cloud) cost 10d. In 1396/7 the rector paid William Roch 10s. for thirty-three cart-loads of freestone brought 'from the hill to Woodman-cote'. Stone from the hill was also used to repair roads, for according to an entry in the court rolls for 1529, the tenants of Cleeve had to provide five wagon-loads of stone per yardland. Unknown quantities of lime, sand and gravel must also have been processed and taken from the hill when the need arose.

Settlement

The evidence clearly shows that more people lived on Cleeve Hill in the later Middle Ages than either before or after, until the development of the 'Cotswold Health Resort' at the end of the nineteenth century. They were based in and around four clearly defined communities, which differ from the areas of settlement at any other times in the hill's history: Wontley, Cockbury, Wick and Haymes (all marked on the map on page 43), in

Looking from the common across the former open fields of Wontley

addition to unknown numbers who had built their squatter homes on public land. The small cottages with long narrow gardens, which were recorded for the first time in the seventeenth century, principally in Gambles Lane, are the descendants of such developments. The best documented settlement was Wontley, on the far side of the common. The village lay a short distance to the west of the remains of Wontley Farm. The Cotswold Way runs by the side of the field which has yielded up quantities of medieval pottery.

Until 1623 it belonged to Bishop's Cleeve manor. In his analysis of the Gloucestershire Domesday book, John Moore has identified Wontley as a sub-manor of Bishop's Cleeve. It was of one hide, with arable land for two ploughs, held by a 'riding man' who took messages for the Bishop of Worcester; however the hypothesis still awaits confirmation from other sources. We have no clear record of Wontley until the *c.* 1170 survey which recorded six tenants with half a yardland each, and one vacant yardland, plus a 'new land' paying 8d. rent – an indication of assarting and settlement expansion. Its position in relation to the estate boundary and the common suggests two possibilities for its origins. It could have been a small early

Saxon settlement which was attached to the land granted to the minster at Bishop's Cleeve, thus explaining how it was enclosed by the boundary. Alternatively, it could have originated as a squatter settlement reclaiming its arable lands from the common, and allowed to continue for the revenue it brought the manor. The lack of any Romano-British pottery found in the area suggests a later settlement. In 1299 there were eight tenants, six half-yardlanders plus two who farmed a half yardland and a smallholding between them; the settlement was worth 37s. per annum to the bishop.

Yet behind the seemingly stable picture of this small settlement, there is evidence which points to structural difficulties within the community at a time when it seemed to have been thriving most. In *c.* 1260 the *Landboc* of Winchcombe Abbey recorded the grant of a yardland at Postlip to John, son of Richard Faber (i.e. smith) of Wontley; the grant was witnessed by Richard himself, together with sons William, a clerk (in holy orders), and another Richard. The grant hinted at lack of opportunity in such a small settlement with clear limits to the expansion of its arable land. The Faber family reappeared in the 1299 survey, when two of the other tenants, Richard Cole and Henry Knyt, are named as the woodwards mentioned earlier in this chapter. For the important job of managing Wontley Wood they were excused payment of half their rent.

It may be inferred from such reports that Wontley at no time had more than a handful of families, and so it is easy to understand how later desertion could have been a relatively simple choice based finally on the decision of just one or two family heads. Wontley was abandoned earlier than many other Cotswold deserted settlements. When the king's assessors visited the parish to collect a tax based on one-ninth of the value of sheaves, fleeces and lambs from the harvest of 1340, Wontley (and Cockbury) lay abandoned, destroyed by robbers, and their fields were uncultivated. The tax list also recorded a dearth of peas, barley and oats; a useful indication of the main crops grown by the villagers. The double reasons given for inability to pay should arouse suspicion that these were excuses designed to avoid payment because the village was in decline, rather than a statement of reality. Indeed, the Bishop of Worcester's records do not support abandonment then, for not until 1372/3 do we read that Wontley was unable to pay taxes and rents 'because of death'. Only then can it safely be assumed that its inhabitants were gone, because its pasture was being rented for 10s. per annum. In 1393/4 the rental had been reduced to 6s. per annum, but the continuing value of its wood is reflected in the sale of underwood at 32s. 1d. in that year. Soon after 1394, when the bishop began leasing out his demesne lands in an attempt to increase his income, Wontley was at first included. But in 1437 the land was rented separately as pasture worth 13s. 4d. Then, in 1482 there occurred a major change – the land was 'enclosed with ditches and hedges' to increase its value by taking it out of the common fields and renting it to two Winchcombe merchants, Walter Hykks and

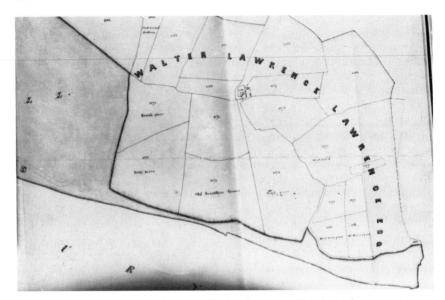

The 1847 Enclosure Map shows well the shape of Wontley's former territory, although West Wood had recently been cleared to its present shape. The darker boundary line confirms that Wontley had never been in Southam manor, despite the late-sixteenth-century claims of the tenants [Gloucestershire Record Office]

Robert Arche, for the exclusive grazing of their sheep, at the vastly increased sum of £6. 13s. 4d. – a rent which stayed stable for at least the next fifty years. We then find the bishop spending 13s. 4d. to put a fence around the wood at Wontley in 1505/6 to protect the underwood from animals straying off the pasture. The attempts by the bishops to increase income in general, and their profits from this small part of one estate in particular, was to the detriment of their tenants. They lost common rights to this pasture. The consequences of the enclosing of Wontley will be followed up in Chapter Four.

The former arable lands of Wontley can be traced today in the landscape, although the medieval ridge and furrow has been ploughed out. Its boundaries still form a distinctive eastern extension of the present Southam parish. Many landowners and tenants can be traced over the succeeding centuries, but they encountered repeated failures to exploit successfully this isolated upland farming area.

In 1327 Wontley was assessed with Cockbury in the Lay Subsidy (a tax based on one-fifteenth of the value of moveable wealth) and between them they had five taxpayers paying a total of 6s. 3d. From this we can roughly estimate Cockbury's population. Since it is usually accepted that only 40 per cent of households were recorded, and Wontley had eight in 1299, therefore Cockbury possessed four or five households. As discussed on page 61, reference to abandonment in 1340 cannot be relied upon, and yet there is very little other evidence for the settlement. One reason for this is that Cockbury was held with Southam manor during this period and like the latter, its records have not survived. It is possible that it was added between 1038 or 1046 and 1086, when Southam's size grew from five to six hides. Certainly *c.* 1170 it was held with Southam by William de Brause. Another reason for uncertainties about its history is that it is not always clear that references to Cockbury are to Cockbury in Southam. During the later Middle Ages it was known as Little Cockbury, to distinguish it from Great Cockbury attached to Winchcombe. Each was recorded as being one hide in extent. It seems likely that the reference to the conversion of seventy-seven acres to pasture by Thomas Escort in 1512 related to Great Cockbury. This led to complaints to the king that two mills had become ruinous, six people had to leave and one plough had been given up. The site of Great Cockbury could be near the present Cockbury Butts.

The geographical position of Cockbury, on the edge of the estate, mirrors that of Wontley and may indicate a similar origin. Its end was probably later than 1340 for reasons discussed over Wontley, but we do not know exactly when, nor by what process. Certainly if the present Cockbury Court stands on the site of the original village – a not unreasonable suggestion given the later history of many Cotswold deserted settlements – the community must have disappeared by the sixteenth century.

Topographical evidence for its arable land still survives today. In addition to the faint ridge and furrow shown on the map on page 43, there is clear evidence that some arable land abutted the north-west boundary of the common, for the change in ground level can be attributed only to ploughing down the slope which lowered the ground immediately next to the boundary.

There is a similar lack of documentary evidence for the small settlement at Haymes. It was always part of the Southam manor but its holders had considerable freedom. In 1299 Adam de Haym, knight, is recorded as holding three yardlands by military service together with his joint tenants. In the 1327 Lay Subsidy Adam le Knyt paid 2s. In 1462 Haymes was recorded with Stoke Orchard in the court rolls. More than that we do not know, except small house platforms lie either side of the present drive to Haymes and much late medieval pottery lies under or near the present mushroom sheds; either or both areas could be the site of the medieval settlement. The ridge and furrow plotted on the map on page 43 represent the arable lands of the village in addition to strips intermingling with those of Woodmancote and Southam as shown on the Haymes estate map of 1731 on page 88.

Faint traces of Cockbury's former open fields can still be recognized beside the B4632. The hedge on the left marks the boundary as recorded in the eleventh century

The smallest of the late medieval settlements on the hill lay at Wick, where the landscape and documentary evidence combine to identify a small settlement of two dwellings clinging to the hillside at the fold of Nottingham and Cleeve Hills. They were approached by two still clearly identifiable tracks off Stockwell Lane. In many ways it is the perfect example of how to locate a lost settlement from a modern Ordnance Survey map, for four footpaths (formerly tracks) meet at its northern end. On older maps 'Wickfield' appears as a field-name higher up the hill slope. Enough survives on the ground to identify the buildings – far more than at the other three sites. It first appeared in the written record in 1299. Walter and Matthew ate Wyke were living there, Walter having the larger holding, paying 8s. 8d., Matthew paying 3s. In 1327 John de Wyke paid 20¾d. tax and Peter ate Wyke 6d. Both entries combined Wick with Woodmancote. The hamlet can therefore be considered as the final phase of the expansion of Woodmancote up the hill. 'Wick' here means an outlying farm.

Once population declined and pressure on land fell, Wick was affected by the retreat of settlement. In 1462 John Fowler was brought before the manorial court accused of possessing a messuage (dwelling house) called Wykens 'which lies badly ruinous and wasted by neglect'. The building had

One possible site of a medieval settlement at Haymes lies either side of the modern drive to the house. The earthworks have been picked out by a light fall of snow

been a small one with two crucks, but it had by then fallen down. Perhaps this marked the end of the settlement as such, although its attendant arable land, clearly surviving as ridge and furrow, possibly continued to be ploughed from Woodmancote for some time after that. The plan of the surviving features (see page 67) clearly shows the remains of two farmsteads on marginal land on the scarp slope. The smallest and shortest lived of the four deserted settlements has produced the best landscape evidence for its earlier existence.

It is clear that the later medieval inhabitants of the hill did not choose to live in these settlements for the view alone, for these were tiny settlements given recordable life by intense pressure of population. As the population fell, especially after the Black Death, the viability of such small communities was then in doubt, and simply because they had been small they had little resilience. In addition the arable land was not of the best quality and all were to a certain extent inconveniently sited for the main centres of community, particularly Wontley. And yet the sites were not totally deserted. The present houses at Cockbury and Haymes represent a continuous habitation on these two sites. Wontley Farm was an early nineteenth-century building demolished in the 1960s, and most interesting of all was

The ridge and furrow associated with Haymes can be seen running under the modern hedge; a view taken from the drive to the house

The former settlement at Wick lies in the centre of this view. Above it, across the centre of the photograph, runs a track from Stockwell Lane to the common. Beyond that can just be identified ridge and furrow

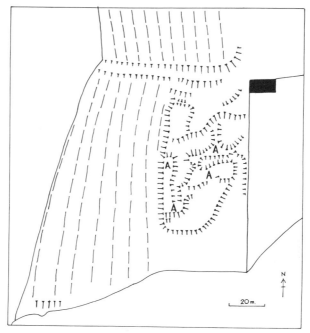

The plan of Wick shows at least four platforms (marked A) on which buildings stood. These are the remains of the two farms found in the documentary record. The trackway and ridge and furrow also stand out [C.C. Dyer]

the small house at Wick, two walls of which still remain. This was last inhabited by an eccentric call Hab or Dab whose name was recorded on the 1839 Tithe Award, but who lives on in local folk memory as one who, in later life, kept his wife in a state of unease by the frequent rehearsal of his own funeral – complete with coffin!

A natural break in the history of the common emerges early in the sixteenth century with the emergence into the written record of Thomas Yardington, a 'socially upwardly-mobile' peasant who took full advantage of the decline of the feudal system and the desire of the bishop to rent out his demesne lands, to become the lessee of the demesne in Cleeve from 1471 to 1525. His attempts to control the grazing on the hill brought him into conflict with the tenants of Southam as everyone suffered from the decision to enclose Wontley in 1482, thereby reducing the common grazing area – a return to the well-established theme of conflict caused by overuse of this scarce land resource.

The appearance of the landscape was now to change little until the end of the nineteenth century, once the arable lands became pasture, except as a result of quarrying. It is therefore to the increasing documentary evidence that we must turn in seeking to understand the use of the hill during the remaining four centuries of its history.

FURTHER READING

The essential context of this chapter is again provided by the two books by Christopher Dyer. *Standards of Living in the Later Middle Ages* contains a valuable section on the peasant economy in Bishop's Cleeve; I am greatly indebted to him for allowing me to use his transcripts of the Bishop of Worcester's records held in the County Record Office at St Helen's in Worcester, reference 009:1. The *c.* 1170 and 1299 surveys are printed in full in *The Red Book of Worcester*, ed. M. Hollings (Worcester Historical Society, Worcester, 1950). The *Victoria County History* Volume VIII again provided background detail.

The 1327 Lay Subsidy was consulted in Gloucester Library. The manorial boundary was abstracted from the Southam manorial records in the Duchy of Lancaster collection DL42 in the Public Record Office in London. The register of Winchcombe Abbey edited by D. Royce in 1892 as *Landboc, sive Registrum Monasterii . . . de Winchelcumba* Volume I (W. Pollard, Exeter) has provided some material on Postlip and Cockbury, but much of the chapter has been based upon fieldwalking, studying Ordnance Survey aerial photographs, and by back projection from the 1731 Haymes estate, 1841 Tithe and 1847 Enclosure Maps held in the Gloucestershire Record Office.

CHAPTER FOUR

Conflict in the Community
(c. 1520–1818)

The hills towards Winchcombe are at present mere downs, lifeless
and unamusing, though the country below is agreeable!
Thomas Dudley Fosbroke, *History of the County of Gloucester*, 1807

Problems of Sources and Contexts

For the next three centuries the face of Cleeve Hill changed little. The
common was established; quarrying barely nibbled at the exposed limestone
beds; the scarp slopes had developed into small irregular fields and areas of
remnant woodland; animals grazed the grasslands, and human habitation
remained unobtrusive to the observer in the vale. During these years the
landscape itself provided the essential continuity, as background to the
turmoil and strife recorded in the written word. The period's unity is based
upon the importance of the common to the manorial economies of Bishop's
Cleeve and Southam; a period ended by the arrival of Cheltenham races in
August 1818.

Superficially another unity can also be discerned in this period: the
context of the hill appeared more localized than at any period before or
since, as both Bishop's Cleeve and the larger part of Southam manor passed
from distant into more local hands. With the decline of monasticism in the
sixteenth century, Bishop's Cleeve manor passed to Queen Elizabeth in
1561. After her death, it was granted away again in 1604 to a succession of
mostly local owners. It changed hands quite frequently and as it did so, its
lands were sold off, so that by 1773 little land remained attached, and by
1885 only the manorial rights. Unfortunately these factors prevented the
accumulation of a body of manorial records for the historian to use.
Consequently the story of the Bishop's Cleeve parcel of the common has to
be pieced together from fragmentary references in other sources. Chief of
these are the Southam manor records.

After the division of the latter manor, first clearly recorded in 1165, the larger part – represented today by the Pigeon House complex of buildings – came to the future Henry IV by his marriage in 1380/81 to Mary de Bohun. From his succession to the throne in 1399 until 1604 the manor remained Crown property. It was again sold in 1609, to Richard Delabere and again in 1833 to Lord Ellenborough. Such continuity of ownership led to a substantial collection of manorial records, now held in the County Record Office in Gloucester. When Lord Ellenborough was negotiating to purchase the smaller part of Southam manor (represented by Manor Farm) from the Coxwell-Rogers family, in order to possess the whole of Southam manor by 1833, he insisted on a search of all the known records to establish their right to title and therefore to sell. Copies were made of many of the records and these, too, are kept in the County Record Office although some of the originals are now lost.

From these manorial records it is possible to gain an impression of the hill and its common in the local context, but it is necessary to look at the events of these three centuries with reference to the wider world which, towards the end of the period covered by this chapter, brings with it a new development encapsulated by Thomas Dudley Fosbroke, whose words at the head of the chapter are the first recorded comments of the visitor seeking out the hill for its scenery and air. By 1807 the growing number of visitors to take the spa waters in Cheltenham demanded a variety of attractions. One of these was a tour of the surrounding countryside. Southam, Winchcombe and Sudeley lay on one tourist route. The visitor could not avoid Cleeve Hill, but theirs was a superficial interest based on fashionable ideas of scenery. As will be discovered, 'lifeless and unamusing' were particularly inappropriate descriptions of the common during these years.

Fosbroke and other writers provide the most obvious reason why the hill became more widely known than in the immediate environs of Bishop's Cleeve and Southam. Yet their interest was just an indirect result of a far more important development – a general growth in population. From approximately two million in 1500, the population of England grew to five million in 1700 and to eight million by 1801. Although outbreaks of famine, disease and depression meant rates of growth were not consistent, particularly in the sixteenth and seventeenth centuries, the underlying upward trend led to increased demand for food. Livestock rearing became very profitable, to provide meat for the markets and manure to feed the soils in areas of mixed or arable farming. Communal grazing on the open fields and particularly on the lowland commons and wastes came under pressure. The problems this created in the early modern period have been summed up by Professor Joan Thirsk in the following words:

> Complaints from villagers all over the country against John Brown and Henry Smith who overcharged the commons with their herds and flocks . . . kept more stock on the commons in summer than they could support

in winter on their home grounds. The complaints were all of one kind, recording the resentment of the many at the selfish ambitions of the few.

The Common as Grazing Ground

For John Brown and Henry Smith we must substitute the names of Sir John Huddleston of Southam House and Richard Southall, who held a house and land in Woodmancote. In October 1539 Sir John accused Richard of trespassing on the common open fields of Woodmancote and Southam, by grazing there over two hundred sheep and an unknown number of cattle. He had already sent his sons to impound the animals, and they used such force that Richard Southall complained that many had had to be destroyed. However, that Richard's motive was personal, commercial profit was strongly suggested when he denied the existence of a two sheep per acre stint, and he blamed the action on a personal grudge held by Sir John. The case could not be resolved at Southam Manor court, and so it was taken to the Duchy of Lancaster court, where the finding went against Richard Southall, declaring he had no rights of common and was therefore a trespasser.

What effect the ruling had we do not know and we do not know on whose behalf Sir John Huddleston acted. We might suspect it was to protect his own interests in grazing animals on the fallow field, but the case set the tone for a long series of court cases over grazing rights on the common between the tenants of Bishop's Cleeve and Southam. To these cases we now turn.

Christopher Dyer has already traced the upward mobility of the Yardington family in Bishop's Cleeve during the late fifteenth and early sixteenth centuries. Thomas Yardington had been only a customary tenant holding six acres of the Bishop of Worcester. In addition to leasing the bishop's demesne in Bishop's Cleeve from 1471 to 1525, he held various official posts in the manor, including reeve, bailiff and juror. In 1541 his namesake son took on the demesne lands and had risen to yeoman status.

At Easter 1563, when both Bishop's Cleeve and Southam manors lay in Queen Elizabeth's hands, we find a Richard *Yerrington*, whom it is reasonable to suppose was of the same family, accused in the Duchy of Lancaster court of preventing Southam tenants from commoning on *Cleeves* Hill by impounding cattle grazing at Barnard's Cross (where the White Way crosses the top end of Dry Bottom). Yerrington rested his case on the whole of the common belonging to the manor of Bishop's Cleeve. Although the tenants of Southam intercommoned freely with their animals, it appears that Richard sought to have their rights removed by playing with definitions. He insisted he knew the hill only by the name of Cleeve Hill, not Cloude nor Covere Clowde. This was only half the truth, for the latter

Barnard's Cross can be found where the White Way cuts the top of Dry Bottom, or
Chappmandeane

names referred exclusively to the Southam portion of the manor, to the south of the boundary markers. He must have known this but was relying on the ignorance of the duchy's officers of the local situation, in order to gain a ruling to deny Southam tenants rights to any part of the hill.

The case smacks of an attempt to claim exclusive rights for the profit of one set of Her Majesty's tenants against those of the neighbouring manor. But the Southam tenants were well prepared. They produced a plan showing the boundaries of the common (which was last known to be hanging on a wall in Southam House early in the nineteenth century) and the two articles of 1482 and 1483 by which the Bishop of Worcester enclosed Wontley for sheep pasture. The court accepted the evidence of these documents and found that Southam cattle had been wrongly impounded and that Southam tenants should enjoy exclusive rights to their part of the common. An order was also made to throw open Wontley for Southam tenants' animals and, once that had been done, Bishop's Cleeve tenants would be able to intercommon upon the Clowde, i.e., the Southam part of the common.

But that was by no means the end of the case. Wontley, of course, still remains enclosed to this day. Its subsequent history is traced later in this chapter. The decision, although technically correct, reaffirmed that the few wealthier and more businesslike freeholders and copyholders in Southam enjoyed grazing rights to two-thirds of the common, confining the much larger number of Bishop's Cleeve tenants to the northern third. What had been won in law had not been won in practice. Before the end of the year Bishop's Cleeve tenants were back in the duchy court. The record of these proceedings throws much light on attitudes towards this precious land resource of lowland England, and provides a classic example of Professor Thirsk's generalized observation.

Richard Yerrington renewed the attack on behalf of the Bishop's Cleeve tenants. Their anger and sense of injustice can be gauged from their language, carefully recorded by the courtroom clerk. The Southam tenants had won the judgement by being better organized and better informed. The three leading freeholders, Edward Wallwyn, the farmer (i.e., lessee) of the manor, Kynnard Delabere, father of Richard who bought the manor in 1609, and William Lorenge of Haymes – speaking, it was claimed, on behalf of themselves and no more than a further two freeholders and nine copyholders – had 'of their covetous mind' claimed exclusive rights to the common for their own profit and for those of their heirs and tenants. They had produced records, court rolls and evidence to support their case, which the 'poor plain men and only copyholders' of Bishop's Cleeve had not been able to counter, their counsel being 'not suitably learned'. Thus at a stroke the traditional common rights 'for the time being time whereof no remembrance of man is to the contrary' were granted exclusively to the Southam profiteers 'to the utter undoing of fifty of the queen's majesty's tenants of the said manor of Cleeve and their wives and children without your pitiful consideration thereof'. These latter had now, however, themselves found an old court roll book of account and other documents dating back to Edward IV (1461–83) proving the freehold of the common was part of Bishop's Cleeve manor, and they wished the case to be reopened.

Underlying the case we can perceive the search for economic profit by the few in Southam conflicting with the greater economic necessity of the many from Bishop's Cleeve. They relied on the common to graze sufficient animals to keep their arable fields fertile but leadership of the community lay in their own hands, being a village of many smaller farms, and they thus lacked the ability to put forward a good case in law. However for their part, they were also only intent on using the law to their own advantage for they had just ignored the 1563 judgement. We know this from questions put to John Garne, of Bishop's Cleeve, when the case reopened the following summer. His replies, even as written down, are a mastery of evasion. He knew Cover Cloud and Nutter Wood and Bentley belonged to Southam but the rest of the common he knew belonged to Bishop's Cleeve. He had heard of the 1563 judgement only through his neighbours. He had no idea by whom and upon whom the decree was issued. He did not know the names of Bishop's Cleeve tenants who had interrupted Southam tenants, but he did know Southam tenants had been fined at Bishop's Cleeve manor court for trespassing on the common. When first asked whether he knew the Bishop's Cleeve tenants were taking out a writ against Southam tenants in the duchy court he only admitted to the possibility and claimed ignorance of its cost. On being pressed further by the duchy's sergeant at law, William Fleetwood, he changed his answer and we discover he had already contributed five shillings to the estimated £50–60 bill for the case. This was all too much and he then refused to answer any more questions. Silence was the best defence in portraying Bishop's Cleeve tenants as the injured, but not innocent, party, and no further witnesses were called. Whatever the outcome of the case (and this is not known), the tenants of Bishop's Cleeve and Southam continued to graze their animals exactly as they had been doing for centuries.

The records of this case, still carefully preserved in the Public Record Office in London, provided a point of precedent for further similar disputes as the conflict between Bishop's Cleeve and Southam tenants periodically spilled into the courts during the next two hundred years. Significantly none ever again questioned the existence of the boundary, but rather the rights over the two separate parcels.

The duchy court rolls record another complaint by Southam tenants in November 1591 before the 1563 case was repeated almost exactly in May 1593 and January 1594. Both cases were pressed by Southam tenants against Bishop's Cleeve tenants overstocking the common and trespassing with their animals on the Southam parcel of the common. In January 1594 the complaint was not only against the overstocking of the Bishop's Cleeve tenants but also against the appearance of fourteen or fifteen hundred 'strangers" cattle on the common. These were animals of people living outside the manor in places lacking communal waste land who had made some sort of agreement with the Bishop's Cleeve tenants to stock their animals on the common. This private economic gain was once again perceived to be to the ultimate detriment of the whole community. The continuing enclosure of four hundred acres at Wontley made the problem of overgrazing worse.

This scrabble to claim grazing rights over commons at this time was not confined locally to the villages of Bishop's Cleeve and Southam. We only need to look over the wall of West Down into Sevenhampton. Before enclosure in 1814 Sevenhampton also possessed communal grazing land on West Down. In 1581 the lord and tenants disputed their respective rights to their narrow strip of common. Theirs was resolved by dividing the length of the common into two even narrower strips by the digging of a line of holes parallel to the existing wall to act as a dividing line: to the north of the line the tenants had their rights of common; to the south, the lord.

One major cause of the continuing conflict over pasture rights on Cleeve

Common lay in the inability to fix and enforce any stinting of animals based upon an agreed ratio of animals to acreage of tenants' arable land in the vale. As mentioned in the previous chapter, in the thirteenth century twenty acres gave grazing rights for two oxen, a cow and calf, and in 1538 in Bishop's Cleeve a peasant yardland gave rights to graze thirty sheep. Such arrangements were recognized only in their breaking, for during the period of these disputes no stinting seems either to have existed or have been enforced. Surveys of the manors in 1620 and 1631 explicitly stated that stinting did not exist. Not until May 1695 do we possess further evidence of attempts to stint the common. Eighty-five freeholders of Bishop's Cleeve (seventy-nine male and six female) agreed to contribute to a High Court action to introduce stinting on the common and in the common arable fields because 'foreigners' were buying an acre or two of land in the parish in order to put cattle on the common, to the prejudice of the locals. The lack of stinting enabled these outsiders to graze limitless numbers on the common. Now not only was the community suffering at the hands of the individuals intent on personal gain, but these individuals were outsiders whose only interest seems to have been personal economic gain. We are not surprised to learn that Southam tenants then agreed to meet the costs of another case in order to establish *their* rights to the common. The Bishop's Cleeve–Southam feud continued just below the surface. It had last boiled over in 1666, but, as before, it continued to be impossible to prevent intermingling of animals on the common.

Although no reference to the outcome of this High Court bid has been found, the case was important because it revolved around that development first recorded (but no doubt of much older origin) in 1594. This concerned the overgrazing of the common by the animals of 'strangers' or 'foreigners' – people with little or no claim in the land of the two manors. It is here in this traditional world of pre-industrial agriculture that we can discern the seeds of a conflict of interest which became all important in the later nineteenth century and which still finds echoes today. This is a conflict between those who wished to continue their traditional use of the common and who were opposed to outsiders, particularly in the nineteenth century from Cheltenham, whose demands ran totally counter to the commoners' rights.

Overstocking continued to be a problem. The clearest indication of the difficulties of enforcing stinting can be found in 1749 when some of the Southam landowners complained that overstocking meant the common had little value for them. Counsel could not give any opinion for the reason that there was no way of being able to enforce any judgement. The tenants were being ordered to act against their own interest and in the continuing absence of any enforcement officer not unsurprisingly carried on as before. Just how valuable were such rights to the common can be measured from two later examples. Firstly in the mid-seventeenth century there was a dispute whether occupation of Cockbury brought rights to the common. In the mid-eighteenth century it seems to have brought rights to the common on Nottingham Hill, and the mention of the right to graze two hundred sheep there suggests some form of stinting. When Lord Coventry gained Great Cockbury in Winchcombe and made an attempt to claim rights over Cleeve Common in 1749 the freeholders of Bishop's Cleeve, gathering together in a vestry meeting, prevented him from doing so. Rights to the common were purchased for Little or Huddleston's Cockbury at about this time. Secondly, in November 1770 Henry Harvey from Winchcombe was accused in Southam manor court of stocking the common without any right. How many others went unrecorded or even unnoticed? Surviving records show it is possible to identify this use of the common as pasture as its most important function. Indeed, when Revd Thomas Rudge published his county history in 1803, his first reference to the hill was to its excellent sheep pasture.

The themes running through this period – litigation, stinting and over-exploitation – are symbolic of the main theme that runs throughout the history of Cleeve: the conflict arising from the interests of inhabitants who defended their own rights and attacked the rights of others, which gives some coherence to our attempt to understand the development of the landscape. Until 1818 these interests were almost exclusively based on the common's value to the local community and society.

Quarrying

The rights to pasture were enjoyed by the tenants but the rights to exploit the land's minerals remained with the lord. Partly as a result of the lack of manorial records, and partly because the quarries seem always to have been worked on a small scale by individuals, there exist very few records of them until later into the nineteenth century. Consequently it is necessary to fill in the gaps between the isolated references with assumptions that small scale workings continued across the hill. The lack of any references to the damaging of the pasture by the spread of quarrying suggests that this was so. Even at Cleeve Cloud the actual workings seem to have been on a small scale, for in 1620, when Southam tenants were allowed to take away freestone for building, it was worth only £1 to the Delaberes. In 1714 Abel Wantner referred to the 'great quarry of freestone' at Cleeve Cloud in the notes for his unpublished history of the county, which is still lying in the Bodleian library in Oxford. By 'great' he was presumably referring to its appearance rather than meaning the scale of exploitation. Freestone was the best quality stone, used in Bishop's Cleeve church at least from the twelfth century; the former Bishop of Worcester's palace from the thirteenth century; and in the Southam Delabere from the early sixteenth century.

Local roadstone was inferior stone dug over the top of the hill, particularly above Dry Bottom. The quarry where the golf club keeps its maintenance gear is, in fact, called Roadstone Quarry.

The fullest continuous record of the exploitation of these quarries during this period can be found in the church wardens' accounts for Bishop's Cleeve. From the early eighteenth century periodic payments were made for the purchase and hauling of stone, lime, slates and gravel from the hill for use in the church and churchyard. These confirm the lack of a regular demand for the minerals, and highlight one major problem. The cost of hauling nearly always exceeded the cost of the stone.

In 1705 stone costing 2s. cost 8s. to haul from the hill. In 1719 fifteen hundred slates were bought at a cost of 13s. 9d., but it cost 10s. to bring them to the church. In 1840 a load of gravel cost 19s. 6d. at the hill, but £4. 11s. 0d. to haul it, again to the church. Lime burning was expensive. In 1723 it cost 19s. 2d. to buy coal and haul it from Tewkesbury. In the same year 3s. was spent on two barrels of Bristol lime, presumably because Cleeve Hill lime was unsuitable for some purpose. We can readily imagine the difficulties not only of loading and carrying the minerals across the steep, narrow tracks of the common itself, but also the severe problems of braking horse-drawn wooden carts as they slithered and slipped down Stockwell Lane and Gambles Lane. Even the main route down to Southam must have caused similar difficulties.

The upkeep of Bishop's Cleeve church, itself built from Cleeve Hill stone, provides us with some of the most detailed records of the quarrying in the eighteenth century

Such references do not provide a comprehensive history of quarrying but they indicate its general nature and confirm that in the early modern period exploitation of the minerals coexisted with the demands of animal grazing and were not the source of conflict they were to become later.

The only other clear reference we have to quarrying concerns Postlip Quarries. The *Valor Ecclesiasticus*, the great survey of the lands of the Church just before the Dissolution of the Monasteries, states that Winchcombe Abbey was still paying 6d. each year to the Bishop of Worcester for these quarries. The need for Cotswold stone in Winchcombe from such convenient quarries meant a continuing demand. Even after the Dissolution in 1540 the demand continued. Some uses are instantly recognizable, such as the cluster of buildings at Postlip itself, dating back to the twelfth century; and in Winchcombe the early seventeenth-century Jacobean House, and the multitude of humbler cottages lining the main streets, received a cladding of Cleeve stone over their original timber framing. This extensive exploitation of the stone in the eighteenth and early nineteenth centuries must have made Postlip Quarries unusually profitable at that time. This can be further inferred from a reference in 1749 to the fact that the quarryman, a James Tarren, was renting the quarries from Isaac Bailiss who in turn leased them from a Mr Bruges, described as Lord of Cleeve manor. Three people felt they could profit from them. Interestingly the boundary between Bishop's Cleeve and Southam manors cut through the quarries and both manors could lay claim to parts of them.

Cotswold quarries are notoriously badly documented. As David Bick has shown in his study of Leckhampton Hill, from where a superior type of stone was taken to provide Cheltenham with its major source of building stone, there is little that can be written with certainty of the period before the nineteenth century. This will be followed through in the next chapter.

Woodland

Between *c.* 1520 and 1818 the physical appearance of the hill changed little. The feature which can change the appearance of the landscape the most obviously is woodland. By the end of the Middle Ages a balance had been reached between continued clearance for increased pasture and arable, and the need to maintain supplies of timber and wood for their many uses. During these three centuries the only significant change in the woodland coverage took place off the hill scarps, in the vale just to the north of Southam village, with the clearance for pasture of *Muckmead* coppice in the 1620s. How many people walking their dogs in the fields near Southam realize that this accounts for the oval area completely devoid of ridge and furrow just one field away from Ratcliffe Lawns? The other woods remained, little changing now that their banks had become established features of the landscape. Investigation of the present landscape can help confirm their nature. Thrift, Stutfield (then called Nutt Wood) and Queen's Woods had areas not only of coppiced woodland, largely hazel, but also of timber trees – particularly oak, ash and beech.

Lower down the slopes towards Southam lay areas of wood pasture, while Wontley Wood grew mostly timber trees. In addition trees for timber grew around the manor, mostly in hedges. These numbered 2,500 in the smaller part of Southam manor in 1620. Their value as a manorial asset is indicated by the £1,000 value placed on them. The present landscape confirms the importance of woodland as a valuable resource at that time. The pollarded trees, now overgrown, in the fields above Southam House provide evidence of wood pasture. This was an attempt to balance woodland and animal grazing where there was pressure on land, for it allowed coppiced wood to grow above the heads of hungry cattle.

These landscape indications that woodland was a precious resource are confirmed by the documentary record. In 1537 George Wallwyn, the farmer of the larger (royal) part of Southam manor was accused of taking timber to repair his house and farming implements, and for firewood, to the detriment of the rest of the villagers. In 1591 Reynold Nicholas was accused of allowing his cattle to spoil a hundred young oaks in Queen's Wood; an accusation repeated in 1599/1600, and again in the following year when he,

A remnant of wood pasture planted on former ridge and furrow above Southam House

in turn, accused widow Elizabeth Cockes of illegally cutting timber in Queen's Wood. Reynold Nicholas was the lessee of Queen's Wood for we find in 1613 Richard Delabere exchanged a house and smithy in Prestbury for Reynold's lease of Queen's Wood in order to consolidate the Delaberes' holding in Southam. Fortunately there still survives a survey of Queen's Wood made in 1604, when the manor was originally sold by the Crown. There were rights to the trees (for timber), to the wood and underwood (for tools, stakes and firewood), to herbage (for cattle and sheep) and to pannage (for pigs). The lopping (cutting the top) and shredding (cutting the side branches but leaving the top) of great trees also enabled the trees destined to provide timber to produce coppiced wood in the years before they were felled.

The complex of internal banks and ditches, now much decayed, reflects the divisions of the wood into its different parts. All the woodland was susceptible to the damage caused by intruding animals, but especially coppiced woodland with its many young, tender shoots. Such damage was a constant feature of complaints. In c. 1800 the value of Stutfield Wood was said to have been reduced by two-thirds because cattle had broken in and damaged the growth.

The most important area for timber lay over the common at Wontley Wood. Although inconveniently situated its importance can be inferred from the plea by the townspeople of Winchcombe to Philip and Mary in 1554 not to grant it out with the rest of the manor. That plea was successful. Although there are no comparable references to those of the Southam woodland, we can measure the importance of the timber. In the survey of 1620 which valued the 2,500 oaks and elms at £1,000, the value of one hundred acres of coppiced woodland was valued at £25 per annum. Even over a complete seven year cycle the value would only be £175, only a sixth of the value of the timber, and a measure of the relative economic importance of the two types of woodland.

There is little more that can be said about the woodland in this period. Physically it remained a stable feature in the landscape; economically it remained an important resource for the tenants. Significantly there are no records of any conflict between the much larger number of villagers in Bishop's Cleeve with their much smaller area of woodland, notably Bushcombe Wood, and the smaller number of Southam villagers with their more extensive woodland. The manorial claims to woodland were much clearer than to grazing.

Settlement

The post-desertion history of Wontley is characterized by attempts to make a profit out of an isolated four hundred acre estate. Until 1623 Wontley descended, with Bishop's Cleeve manor which was sold by the Crown in 1604, to Peter Vanlore (merchant) and William Blake (gentleman), both of London. Their purchase included the land at Wontley and the adjoining woodland. We know the land was still used as pasture and was producing the same rental as in 1482, i.e., £6. 13s. 4d. In 1620 the manor was sold again, to Giles Broadway of Postlip, producing a profit to its former owners of £400 on a £2,700 sale. In December 1623 Giles Broadway sold off Wontley to Ralph Cotton of Whittington for £920. He rented it to Thomas Nicholas — possibly the same person who exchanged the lease of Queen's Wood for a house and smithy in Prestbury with Richard Delabere in 1613.

The failure of the owner to make any real profit from the estate is confirmed by a rapid succession of seventeenth-century owners including one John Jenner, described as of Hawling and Wirdhill in Wiltshire; this episode sheds some light on the complicated financial arrangements people were prepared to enter into in order to gain some personal profit. In the case of Wontley ambition always outran realization.

John Jenner paid £1,000 for Wontley in 1674, holding a mortgage from Sir Henry Pollexton, the Lord Chief Justice. However, John Jenner 'soon after broke, and ran away beyond sea so that he could not be foreclosed'. Sir Henry reclaimed the estate and let it to Carew Williams for £40 per annum, which meant Sir Henry received just £29 profit after taxes — a return of 2.9 per cent. In June 1691 Sir Henry died, leaving debts of £1,400 on the property. The next year his executors were approached by Carew Williams who requested a reduction of £10 in rental. They refused and let it at the original £40 to a Thomas Carter. His motives are not known, but it is difficult to imagine they were solely financial for he knew that during the previous sixteen months Wontley had produced only £13. 15s. 11d. profit.

On Lady Day 1701 the estate again changed hands, being sold to William Dodwell of Sevenhampton for £1,000. The annual profit at that date was £20, but there was none for the next twenty-six years because the lands were said to have been without a tenant. However, we do know that in July 1706 a William Maull, described as being of Wontley, supplied William Dodwell with 130 ewes for £40, William Dodwell then paying Maull 3s. a week for looking after them on the common until Michaelmas. Here, perhaps, is the clue to the continuing interest in this estate which always ended as a liability for both its owners and tenants. It gave them rights of access to Cleeve Common for free grazing in the hope of making good profits from the sale of the animals. This would also explain the importance of the narrow tongue of land stretching northwards towards Padcombe as far as the springs, since its use for watering animals was noted by those who delineated the pre-Conquest boundary of Bishop's Cleeve, and its incorporation into the Wontley estate was carefully established in the deeds. Wontley was still part of the Sandywell estate in 1777, when it was being rented with neighbouring Whitehall to William Cox for £350 per annum. In

Cockbury as it appeared in *c.* 1803. The house itself is the building nearest the centre of this pencil sketch, which shows the area before the building of the present main road in 1823 [Vicar and P.C.C., Winchcombe]

the light of its recent history of economic failure this seemed a much more sensible arrangement.

How far did the developments at Cockbury parallel those at Wontley? Although it possessed some similarities with Wontley, it remained a much more valuable and valued estate. The present, largely seventeenth-century, house is one indicator of this. It contrasts starkly with the fragmentary ruins of Wontley farmhouse. As with Wontley, Cockbury was cut off from the main part of its manor, in this case Southam. Another similarity was that it passed through a succession of absentee landowners who bought the property – partly, at least, for the rights attached to it in both Nottingham Hill and, later, Cleeve Common.

Our first picture of Cockbury is provided by the inquisition, or enquiry into his possessions, taken at the death of Sir John Huddleston at the end of 1548. He held Cockbury of the king and it was worth 26s. 8d. per annum.

The description of the estate provided a reason for its continuing value, for it possessed a mixed economy unlike the single dependence at Wontley upon pastoral farming. The inquisition listed a house, 60 acres of arable, 40 acres of meadow, 60 acres of pasture, 12 acres of wood and 3 acres of moor and heath. It was a microcosm of the balanced estate. As such, its potential value attracted continuing interest which led to its subsequent descent becoming even more complicated than that of Wontley.

The Huddleston family became the owners of Cockbury and in 1609 they sold it and their estates at Guiting for £1,800 to John Stratford, described as salter of the City of London. John Stratford was the youngest of five sons of the Stratford family of Farmcote. Following countless younger sons he had left home as a teenager to seek his fortune in the city of London at some time during the 1580s. He entered the salt trade as an apprentice, then became a member of the London Salters' Company. Always with an eye open to develop his business, John dabbled with importing flax from the Baltic companies in *c.* 1601 with such success that in two years his initial capital of £200 had increased to £1,200. In addition, he developed businesses in tallow, potash, soap ashes and oil; all part of a salter's business. In danger of over-stretching himself, he began to sink some of his capital into more secure investments, and his Cockbury purchase was made at a time when he had begun to buy land not too distant from the family home in Farmcote. In 1621 he was joined in this venture by another salter and a lawyer, both from London. The next year they sold out to another London salter and a merchant, who were then joined in 1627 by two more salters, a lawyer, a merchant and a gentleman, all from London. Ten years later they all sold out to William Rogers of Dowdeswell for £1,119. 6s. 8d. The importance of such 'foreign' capital for the area at this and in subsequent years provided a powerful stimulus for change, and its presence warns against taking too parochial a view of the evolving landscape.

It is clear that part of the interest in Cockbury in this early modern period lay in those rights to common pasture already examined in this chapter. By 1630 the sixty acres of arable recorded in 1548 had shrunk to sixteen acres, tilled in two lots, one for wheat and the other for barley. In that year Timothy Gates, rector of Bishop's Cleeve, took a lease of Cockbury for seven years, paying £55 per annum. The land was valued for its pasture: it could support sheep, and conversion to arable was prohibited on pain of a £5 per acre fine. Timothy Gates was a wealthy man who had bought the manor of Bishop's Cleeve with its manor house (the former bishop's palace) in 1624. The purchase had included forty-six acres in Wickfields. Cockbury adjoined Wickfields so it made sense to have a continuous block of land on the hill. Then in 1641 Gates sold Wickfields to William Rogers of Dowdeswell for £330. As Rogers had bought Cockbury four years earlier at the end of Gates' seven year lease, *he* now had the continuous block of land. Wickfields at that date was described as pasture but recently arable. These are the only fragmentary references to the lands of the deserted settlement of Wick in this period. It is very probable that these fields have never been ploughed since 1641.

Cockbury then descended with the main part of the Rogers' Southam estates until purchased by Lord Ellenborough in 1833. It was an investment for the absentee Rogers family and tenanted by a succession of local farmers. It is fortunate that the survival of many relevant records in the County Record Office gives a fairly detailed picture of Cockbury during some of these years. In 1680 William Rogers leased the farm to John Ballinger. When the latter's widow died in 1724 she owed £550 in arrears in rent. As compensation Rogers took her moveable wealth which was listed in an inventory, or list, taken of her possessions. It is printed on page 86 together with this transcription, because the information it contains provides us with a rare snapshot of an early eighteenth-century farm. The list was drawn up and valued by her sons and the landlord, so we can have confidence in its accuracy.

An Inventory of ye Cattle Goods & Chattells of ye Widow Jane Ballinger as appraised ye seventh day of Nov(embe)r 1724

	£	s	d
Imprimis Money in Purse and wearing Apparell	5	0	0
320 Sheep	128	0	0
035 Cows Heifers & Yarlings	100	0	0
13 Horses & Colts	080	0	0
Eight Piggs	005	10	0
Six Stocks of Bees	001	10	0
In Sawcomb's Barne One Oat Rick One Barley Rick & One Bay of Oats	30	0	0
In ye Grounds Six Hey Ricks	50	0	0
In ye Upper Barn at ye House two bay of Barly one Barly Rick and One Wheat Rick	80	0	0
In ye Lower Barn at ye house two bays of Pease & Rye Grass and three Loads of Wheat	40	0	0
Wool 36 Tod	25	0	0
Two Waggons two Carts two Ploughs 10 pair of Gears Seven Harrows 7 Horse Pads 5 Ox Tows & Yoaks	26	0	0
In ye Kitchen eight Kettles 3 Brass Pans 3 Brass Pots 17 dishes of Pewter 4 plates a Bason 5 Porringers 12 Spoons two pair of Tongues & a Fire Shovel a Cliver & Pot hooks & Links et(c)	7	0	0
In ye Brew house 12 Barrells a Cheese Press and Brewing Tubbs & Skeels et(c)	3	0	0

In ye Rooms above stairs nine Beds & Bedsteads	⎫			
4 Tables 13 pair & one sheet 12 Napkins ten	⎪			
Towells 5 Table Cloathes five Coffers a Clocke &	⎬	20	0	0
Clocke case 12 Chairs et(c)	⎪			
12 Baggs	⎭	0	16	0
23 Blanketts & Ruggs		5	0	0
Eight hundred of Cheese		8	0	0
Tot(al)		614	16	0

as appraised by us
The mark of W[illia]m W Ballinger
Tho[mas] Ballinger
John Rogers Jun[io]r

The picture that obviously emerges is of a prosperous tenanted farm producing wealth for both the tenants (the Ballingers) and, through the rental, to the landlord (the Rogers family). The inventory was drawn up after harvest but before much of the produce of the land was consumed, so that we see the farm at almost the richest time of the year. The greatest wealth lay with the animals, with a total value of £314, and the importance of the rights to common grazing emphasized by the possession of 320 sheep. They had created further wealth in the thirty-six tod (i.e., seventy-two stones) of wool valued at £25. The cattle were obviously largely for rearing, although they provided milk for the cheeses recorded in their usual storage place – the bedroom. The pigs and bees provided meat and honey for the home. Although the gear for oxen was recorded, the only beasts of burden were horses, which is perhaps surprising and represents either an early move to horses or the fact that the oxen on the farm did not belong to Jane Ballinger. The numbers of animals recorded here in the late autumn give the lie to the commonly accepted idea that the animals were slaughtered in the autumn.

The value of the stored crops came to £233 if we include the wool and cheese, £200 if we do not. Oats, wheat, peas and barley (for brewing) were grown in quantity; hay and rye grass had been cut for animal feed. Earlier, in 1630, only wheat and barley were recorded; later in 1774 only wheat and rye, but we do not know how complete these records were, except that the lease taken out in 1774 makes reference to wheat grown on twenty-one acres. It is clear from a valuation carried out in 1775 that the farm had by then lands in Bishop's Cleeve and Winchcombe as well as Southam. By that date it extended to just over two hundred acres with only forty-three acres of arable growing wheat, turnips and seed corn.

The implements and tools are those necessary to run a large farm, but there is a surprising absence of detailed lists of furniture. The total value was £32. 16s., which included £7 for the kitchen utensils. Why such absence? It could have been, of course, that the furniture had already been nominally

Jane Ballinger's inventory of 1724 [Haines and Sumner, Gloucester] passed on to the family. The lack of any furniture recorded in downstairs rooms might support this. However a more likely explanation could be that some of the furniture came with the house. This is indicated in the original lease taken out by Jane Ballinger's late husband John in 1680. It included a list of furniture: a cupboard and table board (i.e., just the table top) in the inner chamber; a bedstead and a wainscot in the outer chamber; a table, bench, form and side cupboard in the hall (main room). If we assume these, or their replacements, were still in the house in 1724, we have a not untypical quantity of furniture for a farm like Cockbury. Even so, to modern minds it appears to have been unbelievably spartan, but tenant farmers were only just entering the world of conspicuous consumption based on continuing demand for food as the Industrial Revolution gained pace in the second half of the eighteenth century. Perhaps this can help explain why the annual rental increased modestly from £150 in 1774 to £163. 3s. 8d. in 1801.

The farm continued to be a mixed economy. When William Arkell of Postlip took on the lease in 1774 he was granted permission to extend the arable land by only six acres at Sestons, the area abutting Wickfield Lane on its way up to the golf club house. He was only allowed to plant wheat or rye and had to follow a rotation of three years' plough and two years' grass. He would have to pay £10 to plough any other area. By 1801 the figure had risen to £30 per acre. This was presumably an attempt by the Rogers to maintain an emphasis towards pasture to keep the holding attractive to future tenants. Thus Cockbury succeeded where Wontley failed, in providing landlord and tenant with a profitable income.

But what was happening to that other late medieval deserted settlement at Haymes? The estate here was held as a freeholding of the larger part of the manor of Southam. In 1610 Thomas Lorenge acknowledged the over-lordship of Richard Delabere for 120 acres by the token payment of 11s. 5d. per annum and the traditional pound of pepper. Thomas was actively adding to his estate, having recently purchased the enclosure at the top of Gambles Lane called Bittemoor. The Lorenge family continued to add to their estate, purchasing valuable meadow land in Prescott by 1631 and coming into possession of the Town Meadow along Dean Brook in Bishop's Cleeve by 1671. In 1675 Thomas settled his lands on his son Charles. By 1679 the estate had grown to 150 acres of arable with 50 more added shortly afterwards; 100 acres of pasture, with rights to the common; and 50 acres of meadow. By then, however, Charles Lorenge had overstretched his finances. He had mortgaged his estate to provide capital and debts had mounted to £3,860 by 1685. In 1688 Thomas was killed at Cirencester fighting for James II. Four years later Charles sold Haymes to Thomas Gooding, a lawyer of Grays Inn, London, for £3,300, thus ending over three hundred years of its association with the Lorenge family by the introduction of yet more 'foreign' capital into the area.

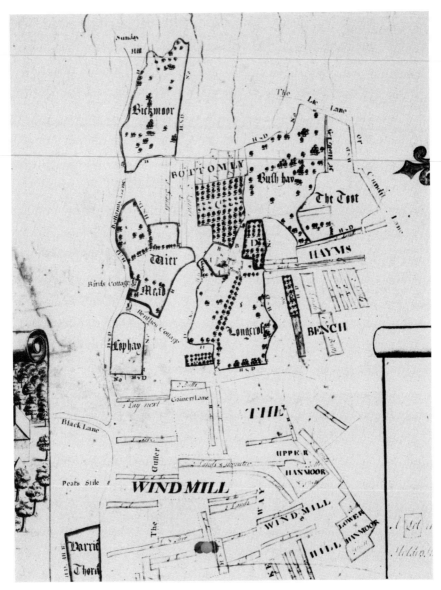

Haymes estate in 1731 [Gloucestershire Record Office]

An aerial view of the same area taken in 1969 [Reproduced with the permission of the Controller of Her Majesty's Stationery Office © Crown copyright]

Gooding continued to develop the estate, enclosing fifty acres from the open fields by 1717, when he settled the estate on his daughter Margaret for her marriage to William Strachan, living at that time in London, but described by Samuel Rudder in his county history of 1779 as 'a baronet of Nova Scotia'. Strachan took up residence in Haymes, spreading his local influence by purchasing the residual manor of Bishop's Cleeve in 1735, and trying, but failing, to re-establish a lord of the manor in the village. Haymes was too far out and the Cleeve farmers by now too independent to bow to an outside lord, even though William built himself a private pew in the centre of Cleeve church in 1746. He was, however, more successful in extending his influence around Haymes where he was active in exchanging land to consolidate his estate.

The accompanying map of 1731 provides an invaluable source for the state of the Haymes estate at this date and the appearance of this part of the hill. The comparison with the aerial photograph taken in 1969 gives some indication of the continuities and changes in the landscape over two hundred years. The enclosed pasture fields surrounded by hedges and ditches with clumps of trees dotted around them, as at Bickmoor, Bush Hay and Long Croft, contrast starkly with the ridge and furrow of the lower slopes and into the vale. Here neither the Lorenges, Thomas Gooding nor William Strachan had been able to consolidate all the Haymes land into separate fields, for the gaps in the map between the fields and strips indicate land in the ownership of others, and therefore of no interest to the maker of a map of the Haymes estate. Even on the slopes around Haymes House, consolidation was not complete. It seemed self-evident to landowners in the eighteenth century that by consolidating land to form blocks which could be enclosed, they could be taken out of the communal system of agriculture and become the place for private experiments. Private gain, to the possible detriment of the community, seemed more acceptable in the arable fields than on Cleeve Common. This can be seen at Bottomley where part of an area of former ridge and furrow was already planted as an orchard.

The detailed view of the house in 1731 provides a unique picture of the earlier building before it was swept away to be replaced by William Strachan's red brick mansion two years later. It looks a typical seventeenth-century Cotswold farmhouse surrounded by its barns. Through the doors of one, a labourer can be glimpsed as he threshes with a flail, and a dairymaid brings in the apples from the orchard. These interesting details remind us that without the countless ordinary people, whose names are never found in the documentary record, there would be no story to tell of Cleeve Hill.

Much of the 1731 landscape pattern remains today, but there have been changes. New Road of c. 1840 now cuts across, as a continuation of Black Lane; the main Cleeve Hill road cuts through Bickmoor and across Lie Lane, and more houses now line Bottomley or Gambles Lane. More importantly, as far as the changing landscape is concerned, the strips of the

Haymes farm and buildings, 1731 [Gloucestershire Record Office]

open fields have been hedged over to create the modern enclosures we call fields. Since the aerial photograph was taken the mushroom farm has changed dramatically the appearance of Haymes as seen from the vale.

William Strachan continued to add to the Haymes estate. In 1754 he bought up one of the cottages bordering Gambles Lane for ten guineas, but the estate was a source of income rather than a holding to be farmed directly, and William got into difficulties when his expenditure, chief of which must have been on the remodelling of Haymes House, outran his income. In 1772 he was declared bankrupt and was forced to sell all his interests in Bishop's Cleeve, including Haymes. Two Worcester gentlemen, John Thorneloe and William Lilly, bought the whole in 1773 for £11,000. The following year Lilly sold his share, which comprised the Haymes estate, to Joseph Cocks, yet another London lawyer, for £3,738. We have no record of how he used the land, except that it seems to have been leased to local people to farm. However the fact that the features mapped in 1731 still remain largely identifiable today, indicates he did little to change the landscape on this part of the hill.

During the Middle Ages the settlement on Cleeve Hill formed small, clearly defined hamlets at Cockbury, Haymes, Wick and Wontley. However, in this early modern period we find the first documentary references to another type of settlement on the hill – the squatter settlement. Families took advantage of encroachments on the common and wide grass verges alongside roads, such as at Bird's Cottage and Bentlies Cottage seen on the Haymes map. The earliest clearly documented example we possess describes a cottage on a plot, near the present donkey stud, in 1582. When Thomas Lorenge bought Bittemoor in 1607 it contained a cottage on part of it. It cannot have been a very substantial building for it does not appear on the 1731 map. In 1693 the bailiffs were sent by the Delaberes to evict a man named King who had built a cottage on the common at Nutterswood. They took swords and pistols, and razed his house to the ground. However, once squatters' rights had been established they remained in people's memories. In 1812 Charles and George Hawker were presented at the manor court in Southam for their encroachment at Nutterswood. Their defence was that they worked the quarries and unlike their predecessor King, they established their right by paying an annual rental of four shillings to the Delaberes. By 1716 the piece of land at the top of Stockwell Lane, where Sheep Way and Emblem Cottage stand, had been taken from the common, which was not then divided by the main road. In that year it changed hands for £26. It was no doubt considered as a future building plot.

Not every encroachment led to building. When Timothy Gates bought Wickfields in 1624 he also bought Oat Piece, that field crossed by the old road to Winchcombe on its way to Postlip. This provides a documented example of a very early encroachment which has remained as a field taken out of the common until the present day. The subject of encroachment will be considered in more detail in the next chapter.

Tobacco and Flax

This later history of medieval desertion sites has been characterized by the interest shown in them by London merchants and lawyers seeking a return for their investments. At a time of rising population and prices, lands at Cockbury and Wontley and the estate at Haymes presented attractive propositions for the purchase of real estate. The present landscape helps us visualize the location of their endeavours, but we would learn very little without the written record. Due partly to the over-ambitious, acquisitive nature of the owners, and partly to the nature of the ground and situation, especially at Wontley, long-term financial success eluded Vanlore, Blake, Lorenge and Strachan. But for one short period some of their investments seemed to have paid off. In the early seventeenth century Cockbury and Haymes saw experimentation in tobacco and flax growing, in a variety of ventures which provided jobs for the poor and income for the entrepreneurs – in the words of Professor Joan Thirsk, 'mutual aid in the Vale of Tewkesbury' (see Further Reading section at the end of this chapter).

The mastermind behind such schemes was John Stratford, the Farmcote lad who had made good in salt, flax and a variety of other trades in the City of London in the years around the end of the sixteenth century. His purchase of Cockbury in 1609, and the subsequent interest taken in it by fellow merchants from London, can be explained as attempts to experiment with new crops. It was truly mutual aid, as they sought to make a profit while giving employment to the many hundreds of poor of the area. In 1619 John Stratford had a hundred acres in Bishop's Cleeve, Winchcombe and Cheltenham. He involved some of the local gentry. We have already met Giles Broadway of Postlip whose daughter he married, Timothy Gates the rector of Bishop's Cleeve, and Thomas Lorenge of Haymes. John Ligon of Arle Court and Sir John Tracy of Toddington were also involved, but the capital came largely from London.

The one year of full tobacco production on the estate was 1619, when good weather and careful cultivation gave work to upwards of two hundred local people between May and November, growing, harvesting and curing the crop. Professor Thirsk has calculated the net profit per acre in 1619 was £26. 9s., compared with £2 per acre for old pasture or meadow. However, at the end of the season the government banned the crop to protect interests in the colony of Virginia. The summers of 1620 to 1622 were cold and wet, and the gentry withdrew, leaving the poor to continue the tobacco growing illegally until it was ended forcibly in 1690; no records have survived which reveal the scale of the later operation.

John Stratford had taken land at high rents on the basis of the likely good profits. He desperately needed another venture and so turned to flax, growing forty acres in Winchcombe and Cockbury. From tending the plant to weaving the linen, he argued eight hundred jobs should be created. It was certainly sensible, for between 1623 and 1627 he claimed the profits had enabled him to pay the £8,000 debts incurred in his tobacco growing venture.

Although such ventures did not, apparently, change the landscape, it is relevant to this landscape study to ask where such cultivation took place. Unfortunately the answer is very difficult to find. The tobacco growing area identified with the Haymes estate amounted to eight acres. It is known from a dispute between Thomas Lorenge and John Stratford, recorded in the Court of Requests in London in May 1621, that only two acres belonged to Thomas Lorenge; the rest was owned by his brother, John. The land was referred to as Conygree Layes which lay in the manor of Cleeve as part of the ridge and furrow in the common fields, and was cut by the common path to Gotherington. Other references to parts of the land as 'Butts' and 'Short Butts' would reinforce the theory that tobacco was grown on the lower slopes of Nottingham Hill, quite a distance from Haymes itself.

At Cockbury land transactions enable us to be reasonably certain that some of the growing of flax took place in the Wickfields, that area of land already referred to, lying at the meeting of the slopes of Cleeve and Nottingham Hills. It is known that John Stratford was growing forty acres of flax at Winchcombe and Cockbury from 1623, and Wickfields itself was forty-six acres, so it is unlikely that the whole of the area was used. It belonged to Giles Broadway of Postlip from 1620 to 1624, when it was sold to Timothy Gates, a time at which John Stratford was struggling financially after the failure of his tobacco venture. In 1622/23 he had paid Giles Broadway three hundred sheep, worth £10 each, to cover his rent. In the following year he paid with twenty hundredweight of flax. It is possible that by selling off large parts of the manor of Bishop's Cleeve, including the manor house, to Timothy Gates in order to raise £3,000, Giles Broadway added Wickfields because Timothy Gates was already heavily involved in these ventures.

It is unclear how long these ventures lasted. When Timothy Gates took on a lease of Cockbury in 1630, only sixteen acres were described as arable, with only wheat and barley growing on the estate – which would suggest flax growing did not take place at Cockbury itself. A further clue that the site of the flax growing was at Wickfields can be found in the agreement drawn up when Gates sold it to William Rogers in 1641. The ground was described as being pasture but had previously been arable, and could have been a reference to the recent flax growing.

Also included in the sale was a 'recently built barn in the close'. Was this the 'Tobacco Barn' of local folklore, lying just off Stockwell Lane and standing in a field called Sheephouse on the 1841 Tithe Map? Certainly the doorway and the coursed rubble stonework at its eastern end look seventeenth-century, but the building appears to have been much altered. The roof has been lowered and the long walls could be nineteenth-century. It is most unusual for a barn to have a doorway, and that in the end wall. Dr J.T. Smith of the RCHM has passed judgement that it is impossible to base any historical conclusions on the standing building. Even if it is accepted that this is Timothy Gates' barn, documentary evidence suggests it was much more likely to have been built for drying and storing flax rather than tobacco.

Early Travellers and Visitors

This chapter has focused on the fact that the appearance of Cleeve Hill changed little over three centuries, and that to understand more fully its life it is necessary to investigate the written record. Although this life can be viewed superficially, in an entirely local context, in reality much of the economy of Cleeve Hill during this period depended upon outside influ-

Tobacco Barn off Stockwell Lane in Woodmancote [T.N. Curr]

ences, chief of these being the necessary demand for food, and capital made in London seeking investment opportunities in the provinces. Hence the continuing interest in Wontley, despite its lack of promise, and experiments in tobacco and flax growing.

However another interest began to develop which was to become increasingly important. Cleeve Hill was viewed by outsiders, such as Thomas Dudley Fosbroke, as a piece of scenery, with little or no awareness on their part of the conflicts and tribulations arising from the varied attempts to exploit its soils and minerals to provide community well being or private profit. The earliest travellers regarded the hill, not unnaturally, as a barrier to progress. John Leland, antiquary to Henry VIII, travelled from Winchcombe to Southam shortly after the end of the Dissolution of the Monasteries in 1540 and was the first to leave a permanent record of his journey 'by good Corne Pasture and Wood but somewhat Hilly', as he wrote in his itinerary. In John Ogilby's *Britannia*, a road book of 1675, the hill was 'a Mile in Height' and the way across it irregular. His accompanying road map clearly shows the continuance of the medieval route along Dry Bottom as part of a long distance way, described in the book as the road from Gloucester to Coventry. It was probably down this track, past Queenwood Grove and down into Prestbury, that five thousand Round-heads had slipped and slithered on their way to relieve the siege of

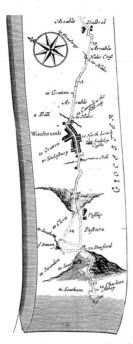

The route across Cleeve from John Ogilby's roadbook *Britannia*, 1675. Prestbury is at the bottom; two routes cross the common, the eastern route being along Dry Bottom

Gloucester some thirty years earlier in September 1643. The night was wet and windy, 'the wind blew a hurricane, the storm descended in torrents'. Most of the soldiers found shelter in Prestbury but the artillery remained on the hill protected by the rearguard. Around midnight the Royalists gave them two alarms, and in the confusion a Roundhead was shot by his fellows. Local folklore has nicknamed the trees known as the Three Sisters (now, of course, only two) as 'Cromwell's Umbrella'. This, however, is another local story unfortunately unsupported by the written sources. Essex, not Cromwell, commanded these soldiers, and the trees in any case are barely half the age they ought to be.

Two other famous people visited the hill before the end of this period. When George III made his visit to the embryonic spa town of Cheltenham in 1788 he travelled to both Bishop's Cleeve and Southam on separate occasions. And Dr Edward Jenner made several visits to a summer house he is said to have built in a wood on the slopes of Cleeve Hill in *c.* 1800, where he collected cowpox matter in his experiments to conquer smallpox.

Queen's Wood was probably the most likely choice as it was reasonably accessible and near pasture ground.

Such incidents give local history much of its fascination, but they are not central to the main theme of change as a result of outside influence. In the years between the visits of these two gentlemen of distinction there occurred a development of much greater importance to the local population. The old routeway across the hill, recorded by Ogilby, was replaced by a turnpike road running across the face of the scarp and traceable today as a bridleway across the common and down Spring Lane. It is shown on the plan of routeways on page 32.

On 1 June 1792 a meeting was held at the White Hart in Winchcombe for the purpose of improving the road system centring on that ancient town. The usual complaints about the inadequacies of the roads for trade were made. As a result the road over Cleeve Hill was turnpiked as part of the Cheltenham to Evesham road. Bars were set up at the Corndean Lane turning near Winchcombe and on the Cleeve Hill side of Southam village just above the present junction with New Road. The list of tolls reflected the usual charges on traffic rather than its local nature – draught animals (horses, mares, geldings, mules, asses, oxen or bullocks) were charged 6d. when in harness, but 2d. when not. Exemptions from tolls not only included the more obvious – mail coaches and soldiers – but also empty wagons, loads of stone for roads, dung, ploughs and people going to church on

The milestone is clearly visible to the left in this view of Cleeve Hill taken at the turn of the century. Tom East is the roadman

Sunday. The order in which the exemptions are listed perhaps gives an indication of the contemporary values of the trustees.

Thirty-one years later the road was lowered to its present line; a move thoroughly acclaimed by the county magistrate, F.E. Witts of Lower Slaughter, who recorded a much improved journey along the new road in an entry in his diary in late December 1823. The trustees had to set up milestones. The present milestone which gives its name to Milestone Quarry dates from this time. It has lost its plate but represents four miles out of Cheltenham and three miles to Winchcombe. Despite the lowering of the route, Cleeve Hill still presented, as it still does present, a major obstacle to travellers. As the need to reach and cross the hill increased in the nineteenth century the problems intensified; they will be discussed in the next chapter.

Finally, the early modern period provides the first visual record of what Cleeve Hill actually looked like. Southam Delabere was depicted in an engraving by Kip for Sir Robert Atkyn's county history of 1712. The hill is shown as a stylized backcloth, yet it is instantly recognizable – Cleeve Cloud

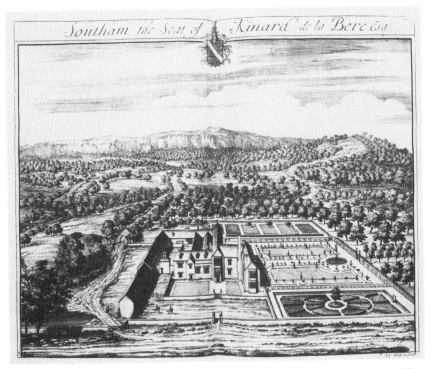

Kip's engraving of Southam House provides the first representation of Cleeve Hill in 1712. Although stylized, many features can be recognized [Birmingham University]

and the Undercliff, with Thrift Wood below, are easily identifiable. So too is the representation of wood pasture and the tracks leading to the summit, even the driftway between Sunset and Bentley Lanes in the left of the print. Kip's engraving is confirmed on many points by Thomas Robins' pencil sketch of the windmill which stood between Southam and Woodmancote. Robins' print is full of fascinating detail: the hunt chasing across the unenclosed ridge and furrow; the heavily laden horse; Haymes shortly after rebuilding by William Strachan (compare this with the earlier house shown on page 91). Again Cleeve Hill in the background is clearly recognizable, while to the right are Cleeve Cloud and Thrift Wood, the hedges dividing off the pasture fields and Gambles Lane twisting to the common. On the common can just be discerned two buildings. This is additional confirmation of the process of encroachment on the common. It is known that by the end of the eighteenth century an encroachment had been made along Spring Lane by William Kitchen, and on this encroachment were built two cottages – probably those seen in the engraving, Pear Tree Cottage and what is now called The Luib. William Kitchen also built a stable: he carried out some haulage of the stone. This was later enlarged and is now called Sunnyside. These seem to be the oldest surviving houses on the hill, their traditional appearance reflecting their close links with the hill and standing in stark contrast to the later mansions and villas reflecting the wealth of the Cheltenham traders a century later.

Pictures can be notoriously misleading as accurate representations of past landscapes, but the visions given by Kip and Robins do seem to agree with

Although a rather poor copy of the untraceable original, Thomas Robins' pencil sketch contains much visual evidence for the hill in the second half of the eighteenth century

the topographical and written evidence that by the eighteenth century the appearance of Cleeve Hill had stabilized into that which would be clearly recognizable today.

The chapter began with a contemporary quotation on the landscape; it ends with another. This comes from Samuel Griffiths' *New Historical Description of Cheltenham*, published in 1826, and aimed at the large number of visitors to the spa. In common with many guide books, he published a series of rides from Cheltenham. One went over Cleeve Hill. The resultant eulogy to the vale contrasts with the travellers' attitude to the hill, reflected in Griffiths' text: it is ignored, except as an obstacle to progress. The description fails totally to appreciate the vital role it was playing in the life of the local community which lay at its feet:

> The boundless beauties of the vale – the ascent of the protecting upland – the appearance of steeples and church towers, uprising like so many landscapes, and the multiplied and countless dwellings that give variety to the wooded plain, through which the Severn, joined by its tributary streams and rivers, runs its impervious course – all the vast tract of country, extending on the one side far into Herefordshire and Worcestershire, and on the other to the bold and formative heights of the Welsh mountains – all combine to form one grand and glowing picture, all life and light, all splendour, immensity and magnificence!

FURTHER READING

Many of the sources have been referred to in the text. Details of Joan Thirsk's articles are as follows: 'Projects for Gentlemen, Jobs for the Poor; Mutual Aid in the Vale of Tewkesbury 1600–1630' in *Essays in Bristol and Gloucestershire History*, ed. P. McGrath and J. Cannon (Bristol and Gloucestershire Archaeological Society, Bristol, 1976) and 'New Crops and their Diffusion: Tobacco Growing in 17th-Century England' in her own *The Rural Economy of England* (Hambledon, London, 1984). She is also editor of *The Agrarian History of England and Wales*, Volume IV (Cambridge University Press, Cambridge, 1976), which has provided a general background to this chapter. D.E. Bick's *Old Leckhampton* (privately published, Cheltenham, 1971) gives a general background to quarrying on Leckhampton Hill. The *Victoria County History of Gloucestershire*, Volume VIII, carries the descent of the manors; and the *Transactions of the Bristol and Gloucestershire Archaeological Society*, Volume 50 (1928) carries an article by Canon Dowdeswell on Southam House and its deeds. Surviving Southam deeds and manorial records are deposited in the County Record Office, particularly collections D1637, D2025 (especially boxes 30/1, 69/70) and D2957. The descent of Haymes has been traced from

D127; Wontley from D444 and Cockbury from D627. Disputes in the Court of the Duchy of Lancaster can be found in the Public Record Office in London in collections prefixed DL1/3/4/6/42, where the Court of Requests case can also be found (Req. 2, Bundle 30/44). This reference is owed to Professor Thirsk.

There is a long account of the Civil War episode in *Bibliotheca Gloucestriensis*, Volume I, in the Gloucestershire Collection in Gloucester Library.

CHAPTER FIVE

Cheltenham Moves Out of Town
(1818–1855)

WEEP Kingscote, weep, thy raining glory's o'er;
Let Bibury boast her matchless sport no more:
Thro' Gloucester's vale let Cheltenham's fame resound,
And prince of courses Cheltenham's course be crown'd!
Cheltenham Races: A Poetical Description, Anon, 1820

The Context

The year 1818 marked a turning point in the history of Cleeve and its common. In that year Cheltenham races were first held on the western approaches to West Down. They signified the arrival of a new and increasingly important influence on life on the hill – Cheltenham moving out of town. From this point onwards our story becomes dominated by the spa town's spreading influence on to this great area of upland common. It was now increasingly seen as an empty open space for the recreational use of the leisured classes and masses who viewed the sheep and cattle as an irrelevance and intrusion. Recreation now became a major new use of the common. Thus in this period the local farmers and freeholders, whose jealously guarded rights provided the driving force of the hill's story over the past thousand years, became marginalized in their own territory, bought off for a few pounds by the fashionable beau monde attracted to the growing spa town of Cheltenham with its multitude of amusements and distractions.

Cheltenham certainly did grow, from approximately three thousand people in 1801 to thirty-five thousand in 1851 and forty-five thousand in 1891. During the 'season' from April to November many thousand more visitors swelled the town, demanding, and receiving, all manner of entertainments and pastimes to while away the dreary periods between bouts of taking the spa waters. Balls, card parties, dinners, plays and concerts attracted the English (and Irish) nobility, the county gentry, and manufacturers and traders who, having made their money in the Industrial Revolution, escaped to Cheltenham to aspire to gentility. They were followed by their servants, hangers-on, and an immeasurable underclass of petty criminals, pickpockets, confidence tricksters and swindlers. Not without cause was Cheltenham described as 'The Merriest Sick Resort on Earth', and when a few local traders decided to add a race meeting to the attractions, choosing Cleeve Hill on account of its open space and good racing turf, the local commoners were submerged by a new influence against which their existing methods of social control were to prove no defence at all. The self-governing vestry meeting in Bishop's Cleeve and the continuing manor courts in Southam had always tried to balance the existing uses of the common for the benefit of the community against the private gain of the individual. They were unable to protect adequately the commoners' right to grazing against the hoofs of the thoroughbred racehorses. They did insist on, and receive – although invariably after a struggle – £30 annual rental from the racecourse Turf Club, but it only really served as a token of their powerlessness and irrelevance in the face of the new modernity flooding in from outside. Their impotence is well illustrated by a further passage taken from the ballad quoted at the head of the chapter:

> With sluggish step departs the surly clown,
> And drives his flock from Cleeve's deserted down;
> The dog's loud bark, the sheep's quick tinkling bell
> Are heard to sound amid the neighbouring dell.

Cheltenham races on Cleeve Hill not only formed an important episode in the history of the hill, but also form part of the history of Cheltenham and the prehistory of its present famous course.

Cheltenham Races on Cleeve Hill

From the radio masts at the west end of West Down it is difficult to visualize the hustle and bustle of an early nineteenth-century race meeting. It is well known that such meetings were held here, but written accounts of them usually form little more than a footnote to the history of the present course at Prestbury Park. But they are entitled to more than a footnote. They stand important in their own right, not only in the history of horse racing but also because they represent the first major threat to the traditional life of the common.

The races formed part of the social whirl of the spa. Their rise and fall mirrored the rise and fall of the attraction, unlike the contemporary meetings at places like Ascot and Newmarket, where the races themselves were the sole focus of the social whirl. A tale much repeated throughout the nineteenth century was that they originated in the occasional sweepstake run for a plate by the horses of the local gentry on the top of Nottingham Hill. Ruff's *Beauties of Cheltenham*, published in 1806, seems to be the earliest guide to carry the story. It has been impossible to be more precise than this.

Until enclosure in 1807, the top of Nottingham Hill lay as unenclosed common land – a favourite place to hold races. From at least 1721 to 1813 races were held on Tewkesbury Ham; and until 1827 races were held on Minchinhampton Common. In 1818 they started on Cleeve.

In July of that year the *Cheltenham Chronicle* announced the intention to revive the races as an added attraction in the spa, should enough subscribers be enlisted for a sweepstake. By the middle of August ten five-guinea subscribers had been found to run a mile race on Cleeve Common, which took place on Tuesday 25 August. The whole meeting was a rather local, rustic affair. It was open only to hacks living within three miles of Cheltenham. The arrangements were organized by Mr E. Jones of the Shakespeare Inn in the lower High Street. Fittingly, it was his five-year-old brown mare Miss Tidmarsh which became the first winner of the Cheltenham races. Three further races followed, and the meeting was declared a success.

Two months later steps were taken to make the meeting permanent and much grander. A public meeting was called at the Town Hall in Regent Street, to open a subscription to lay out a race course and build a stand on Cleeve Common. Alex Fotheringham, Master of Ceremonies at the spa, headed the committee. Baynham Jones, owner of Cambray Spa, John Cossens, the Postmaster, John Gardner, owner of the town's largest brewery, Theodore Gwinnett, solicitor and clerk to the Town Commissioners, and J.D. Kelly, owner of the new Assembly Rooms, all added their support. Colonel Berkeley of Cheltenham's leading family subscribed a thousand guineas to open the list. Thomas Morhall, the town surveyor, was appointed secretary with the task of finding subscribers. The Duke of Gloucester agreed to become the necessary prestigious patron and subscribed a hundred guineas.

Who were the poor commoners of Bishop's Cleeve and Southam to stand up to this onslaught of foreign money and men of weighty provision in order to defend their ancient common rights against the beau monde who were intent on turning their precious resource into an open-air extension of the spa's many amusements?

In vestry assembled in Bishop's Cleeve church, the freeholders demanded some recompense. They were granted £30 a year for the intrusion, by the stewards of the racing club. To the latter this must have been a minor matter in their accounting; they spent in the first year over £400 on improving access to the course and setting it out. Yet they were bad payers. By 1822 they were two years in arrears and the villagers threatened to deal directly

Cheltenham Race Course, showing the figure-of-eight track and the grandstand
[Reproduced from the 1828 Ordnance Survey map]

with the stall-holders at the races if the money was not paid into parish funds. £60 was paid and used to subsidize the local ratepayers in Bishop's Cleeve and Woodmancote, Brockhampton, Southam and Stoke Orchard. Thus the tradition and traditional rights were bought for a small price and their upholders thereby cast as people of little importance in this new and exciting world in which the people who mattered most were those with the largest purses.

A figure-of-eight course was set out at the entrance to West Down; spaces for booths were rented out for five guineas each; balls and dinners were arranged for the evening entertainments; and posters were printed to spread the good news. Racing then took place over three days from 23 August 1819. The big race was the Gloucestershire Stakes over two miles, run on the first day. It was worth 125 guineas and was won by Mr Calley's three-year-old, Champignion, after a good race. The Cheltenham Gold Cup was at this date only the second big race of the meeting, run on the Wednesday. Unfortunately, Thursday was left without a major race, which

A poster advertising the first fashionable meeting of Cheltenham races [J. Tester]

continued to be a problem for several years. The meeting, however, was a great success. The race course was difficult to reach but its turf made for good sport, particularly in this hot, dry summer which had cracked many other courses and spoilt many races.

Yet the venture was not without its critics. Even before the first race, and over eight years before Dean Francis Close published his well-known pamphlets on the evils of racegoing, a lively debate was being conducted in the *Cheltenham Chronicle*. The protagonists argued the races would stimulate better breeding and increase local demands for hay, straw and oats. The antagonists claimed they would encourage 'bad company and profligacy', and pointed out that Waterloo had been won by horses fit for steeplechasing, not thoroughbred flatracers. The economic versus moral argument is a familiar one – and steeplechasing was considered fit only for heavy cavalry horses, not the true racehorses of England. It only gained popularity in Cheltenham after the decline of the meetings on the flat.

What was it like to attend these early races? The day started at The Plough in Cheltenham. From Winchcombe Street a variety of carriages

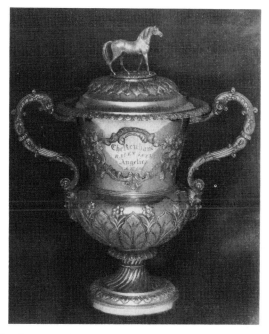

The 1823 Cheltenham Gold Cup. The horse Angelica won 120 guineas for its
owner, Mr West [E. Gillespie]

made their way along Ogilby's road out of Prestbury, covering their
occupants with white dust as they trailed up the hill. On the downs an
amazing sight met the eyes. There was a grandstand overlooking the course,
which was clearly marked by the carriages bordering its length. Behind them
stood booths, sideshows and other attractions. In some years Mr Wombwell's
famous 'Exhibition of Wild Beasts' kept people amused between the races, but
there were always stalls with toys, dolls and gingerbread, gambling booths,
pea and thimble tables, all designed:

> With thousand other idle schemes to drain
> The hard-earn'd savings of each rustic swain!

Pickpockets thrived. In 1825 they roamed in gangs estimated to be up to
two hundred in number, but none were caught and in crowds estimated to
be fifty thousand strong the pickings were easy. Thirty-two carriages are
said to have been stripped in one race alone. The festivities continued after

A seemingly close-run race – the Gloucestershire Stakes of 1826. This is the only
known picture of the Cleeve Hill races [Reproduced by courtesy of Cheltenham Art
Gallery and Museums]

the day's racing. The Turf Club held its dinner on the eve of the meeting; the
stewards held their dinners on each day; there were balls on three nights in
race week and plays on two nights. Cleeve Common just happened to be a
very convenient place for visitors in Cheltenham to amuse themselves
watching horse racing during three days in high summer.

Yet there were always problems associated with holding the races on
Cleeve. Reaching it was one of them, even after the present road lowered the
approach in time for the 1823 races. Three years later the new road from
Cheltenham to London was constructed (now the A40) and patrons were
advised to use that and approach the course via Whittington. In addition the
weather could be bleak when the wind blew and the rain slanted in, as
happened in 1823. There was no shelter and attendances fell. In that year
the first rumblings to move to Prestbury Park were heard, but they came to
nothing for another eight years.

However, towards the end of the 1820s Cheltenham was becoming a
more sober place, as 'The Merriest Sick Resort on Earth' became a hotbed
of evangelicalism after the arrival of Francis Close in 1824. His campaigns

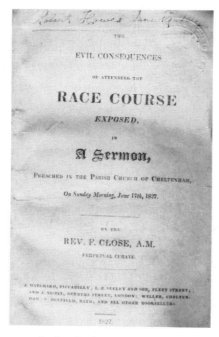

THE

EVIL CONSEQUENCES

OF ATTENDING THE

RACE COURSE

EXPOSED,

IN

A Sermon,

PREACHED IN THE PARISH CHURCH OF CHELTENHAM,

On Sunday Morning, June 17th, 1827.

BY THE

REV. F. CLOSE, A.M.

PERPETUAL CURATE.

J. HATCHARD, PICCADILLY; L. B. SEELEY AND SON, FLEET STREET;
AND J. NISBIT, BERNERS STREET, LONDON; WELLER, CHELTENHAM; T. DUFFIELD, BATH; AND ALL OTHER BOOKSELLERS.

1827

The sermon which started the lively controversy over the races, and which subsequently split Cheltenham in two [Cheltenham Library]

against horse racing, the theatre and political Radicals are well known: 'And this I know, that the roads, and fields and pathways leading to the emporium of vice and folly, are strewed with the victims of vice and vicious excess', he thundered from the pulpit in June 1827, just before the race meeting of that year. The sermon was printed as a pamphlet, sold 4,500 copies within the month, led to a lively controversy and split the town into opposing camps.

At a time when Cheltenham's days as a fashionable spa town were fading it was inevitable that this would be reflected in the races. What could be done? In 1828 the meeting was brought forward to June to be nearer the start of the spa season, but the newspapers reported that the fashionable people were not in attendance, and the crowds were smaller than in previous years. In 1828, in an attempt to improve the middle day's racing, it was decided to incorporate the races from the former prestigious meeting at Bibury which had folded in 1827 – a move, according to the *Cheltenham Journal*, which would enable Cheltenham to rival the great flat meetings of

Doncaster and Newmarket. It was a flop; only two races were run and attendance was very poor. The following year disaster really struck. The grandstand burnt down – aided, whispered some, by the followers of Cheltenham's Dean who continued to launch further attacks on the races. The races could well have folded completely by 1830 if Lord Ellenborough had not offered his newly purchased Prestbury Park to the Turf Club.

There was renewed enthusiasm, not least because the problem of accessibility had been solved. The Jearrard brothers were commissioned to build a grandstand for seven hundred spectators in the hope of attracting the ladies to the course. Paganini, the famous musician, gave two concerts in the Assembly Rooms during race week in order to boost funds. The meeting was cut to two days and while the crowd of ten thousand was said to be satisfactory, the sport was poor. Nevertheless many wondered how Cleeve had ever attracted a second meeting.

Four years later racing was back on Cleeve. The quality of the races at Prestbury Park was far below that of races on the hill, thanks to the latter's superior turf. In preparation the road through Whittington was improved; a new three-storied grandstand, 60 ft long with seating for four hundred on

The 'new' road to the race course through Whittington. It still serves as an entry to the common today

the roof, was built out of Cleeve Hill stone at a cost of £1,200. The *Gloucester Journal* declared they were the best attended races since 1819, but the sport was disappointing. Only ten ran in the Gloucestershire Stakes and only two in the Cheltenham Gold Cup. Despite the best intentions of the stewards the great days of Cheltenham races were fading into the past with the spa which had given them their birth.

Four years after returning to the hill with such high hopes, the races were again in difficulties. On 7 July 1839 the Turf Club held a public meeting to raise funds. The secretary was owed £100 from the previous year and the total cost of £450 for the next meeting had to be met. £200 were raised and the races were able to go ahead, but a securer financial footing was desperately needed. The solution came from opening a three year subscription list to the county gentry, and renaming the races 'The County of Gloucester Races on Cleeve Hill Course'. Strictly speaking *Cheltenham* races had ceased to exist. But interest was not reawakened. The first county meeting took place on 21 and 22 July 1840. There were two races on the first day, and three on the second. Only six ran in the Gloucestershire Stakes, although four of them crossed the line together after an exciting race. The grandstand was full but there was little other life around the course – not even, according to the *Cheltenham Free Press*, any thimble tables.

In 1842 enthusiasm and subscriptions ran out. The nation was gripped in an economic depression. Cheltenham had metamorphosed into a sober, pious centre for education. There was little future for an activity which belonged to the merriest sick resort. Only forty couples attended the race ball; the meeting itself was 'stale, flat and unprofitable' according to the *Cheltenham Free Press*. The report of the last race in the *Cheltenham Examiner* provided a fitting epitaph:

> In consequence of the fog, the whole went the wrong side of the post, and were forced to pull up. They then groped their way in the dark the best manner they were able, and the race was won by *Delusion* by a head.

Two months later the grandstand was demolished. It had cost £1,200; it was sold for £155. The last rental was paid to the Bishop's Cleeve vestry; once again it was late. Two years later only forty people turned up to a meeting in The Plough to consider revival. Racing on Cleeve Hill had ceased to exist, the victim of changing fashions and times. It could not outlive the decline of the spa which had given it its birth – and yet there was to be some life after death.

Away from the genteelness of the flat, the same years which saw the decline of the summer race meeting brought the rise of a spring meeting for the less polished horses of the Berkeley Hunt, as a way of rounding off the hunting season. It was in these rustic cross-country races, not the sophisticated races of the thoroughbreds, that the present Cheltenham meeting had its origins. Cleeve Hill was again involved.

The Cheltenham Grand Annual Steeplechase was initiated in 1834 in Prestbury Park. In 1840 it moved to Andoversford, by which time it had earned the reputation of being second only to the Liverpool Grand National. Seven years later it moved back to Prestbury and for several years was run around the lower slopes of Cleeve. The 1847 race has passed into literary history as the subject of the poem 'How We Beat the Favourite', written twenty-two years later by Adam Lindsay Gordon, once Australia's national poet. He had watched the race as a fourteen-year-old lad. In the poem he described how he beat the favourite ridden by the famous local steeplechase jockey George Stevens, after a hard race. The reality was even harder. The course ran from Knoll Hill to the Hewletts, and it was a hard ride: one of the horses was ridden into a tree and killed. Not surprisingly this route was never ridden again.

The Grand Annual stayed around Prestbury Park until 1855 when Prestbury Park was bought by Mr Dodson of Rose Hill for £19,600 in January of that year. He was determined to bring the racing to an end and so the steeplechase moved to Bibury. At this point the idea of resurrecting the flat racing on Cleeve Hill grew in the minds of the racing fraternity. Thus developed a little-known episode in the history of racing in Cheltenham –

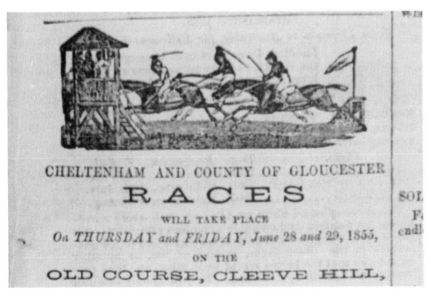

An advertisement for the revived race meeting of 1855. The race representation is stylized rather than realistic [Cheltenham Library]

the 1855 *Cheltenham and County of Gloucester* races run over two days in June on Cleeve Hill. They were a conscious attempt to revive an old tradition.

A race committee was established in May. It persuaded the Duke of Beaufort and Captain Francis Berkeley to agree to become the prestigious stewards necessary to attract the finance and entries. An agreement was reached with the commoners to set out the course on payment of a rent of £20. A temporary grandstand was built; booths and refreshment stalls erected on the course; the Great Western Railway ran the first recorded race special to Cheltenham. Thursday 28 June proved a warm, pleasant day. Five races ran, the sport was good and the grandstand full. A further five races were run on the Friday and they, too, provided good sport, but attendance was poor. It only seemed to confirm that the races belonged to the faded spa years. It was this, rather than the continuing complaints about the route to the common, which meant there would be no revival of the races. In 1856 the Grand Annual Steeplechase returned to Cheltenham and was run along the (old) Gloucester Road; in 1857 it was run around Andoversford; for a period in the 1860s it was run around Kayte Farm on Southam Lane; and since 1902 back at its present home at Prestbury Park.

The story of Cheltenham races and its close association with Cleeve Hill is worth telling because it is so little known. But its context was wider than that of the hill itself and the story could not be told if it were confined solely to that small area. At the simplest level this is because there is nothing left in the landscape, except for the new road from Whittington and a depression near the car park by the radio masts, which might indicate the site of the grandstand. At a deeper level we have to seek out the Cheltenham newspapers and pamphlets to provide us with the evidence upon which to build the story. At the deepest level we have to recognize that the conflict of interest over this use of the common was the result of the development in the wider world of a leisured class intent on its own pleasures, riding roughshod over the interests of the inhabitants of Bishop's Cleeve and Southam who were forced by such outside influences into a position in which they were portrayed as country yokels potentially spoiling the fun of the county society and their hangers-on.

Nowhere is this better exemplified than over the annual £30 payment due from the Turf Club to the vestry meeting of Bishop's Cleeve for the right to hold the races. A minor item in the budget of the Turf Club, it was a major source of income to subsidize the local ratepayers. It was used to contribute to the poor fund, for repairs to the church and local roads, and to defray the expenses of a haywarden appointed from 1821 to look after the animals on the common. The feeling of impotence among the parishioners faced with the alien might of the Turf Club can be gauged from the minutes of the parish vestry meetings. The request to the Turf Club to pay its arrears was an almost annual feature of the minutes, right to the last meeting. The

Captain Barnett's stables, which were added to a house built in a disused quarry on the common in *c.* 1850. Owen O'Neill keeps the historic connection alive today.

commoners had to fight hard to retain their traditional rights to the soil in a widening world in which, increasingly, money had the loudest voice. They, consequently, had none. Cheltenham races had changed the wider perception of the common from its being a vital local resource to being an open-air playground for Cheltenham moving out of town.

The Common as a Training Ground

Thus the races have vanished, but not, of course, the horses. The daily training of tomorrow's hopeful champions provides the continuity with this episode of the history of Cleeve, for the superior qualities of the turf which first attracted attention to the common provide excellent training ground and it is the training rather than the racing which has left its mark on the landscape.

The most obvious feature is created by the stables in the quarry opposite the top of Stockwell Lane. They were built in *c.*1850, by Captain Barnett of

GEORGE STEVENS ON LORD COVENTRY'S "EMBLEM"—WINNER OF THE GRAND NATIONAL STEEPLECHASE, 1861, AND OF THE CHELTENHAM GRAND ANNUAL, 1863 AND 1865.

The caption is mistaken: Emblem won the Grand National in 1863 [P. Jones]

Bayshill Lawn and they were home to William Holman and his five racing sons for over forty years. William Holman won the Cheltenham Grand Annual five times and trained three Liverpool Grand National winners. His first Grand National success was with a horse called Free Trader which won the 1856 race as a 25–1 outsider. The jockey was George Stevens, once a local hairdresser, who had been trained to ride at the stables.

George Stevens enjoys modest fame as the only jockey ever to have won the Grand National five times. It is not a feat which is often included in the history books because steeplechasing in general, and the Grand National in particular, was not, in the middle years of the nineteenth century, regarded very highly by the true sons of the sport on the flat. In 1863, when George won for a second time, he was riding for Lord Coventry. His horse Emblem won by an unprecedented twenty lengths. When he repeated his success the following year on her sister Emblematic, Lord Coventry's reward enabled him to buy a small cottage on a piece of land long stolen from the edge of the common, which he renamed Emblem Cottage. There he set up a small racing stables of his own in 1866. Further success for Stevens in the Grand National followed on The Colonel in 1869 and 1870. In 1871 he rode the same horse into fourth place; he then went on to win the Licensed

Emblem Cottage at the top of Stockwell Lane

Victuallers' Plate at the Cheltenham Steeplechase meeting. This was his last success, for in June he was dead, thrown from his cob The Clown in Southam after it had bolted down the hill when returning from a day at Cheltenham market. A stone marks the spot today. George was thirty-seven; each time he had won the Grand National a bonfire was lit on the hill. From the Spanish Armada in 1588 to its four-hundredth anniversary in 1988 the elevation of Cleeve has made it the logical place from which local people send messages to the wider world.

George Stevens learnt to ride with William Holman; he learnt his tricks from Black Tom Olliver, a larger-than-life character who trained on the hill from his Prestbury stables. 'The post is the place to win at, lie away from the horses' was the advice which won George the Nationals but lost him his job with Lord Coventry who thought he had lost his nerve. Black Tom was always in arrears with his payments to the vestry meeting in Bishop's Cleeve for using the common as training ground. In 1855 he promised to pay the £20 still owing only if the race meeting on the hill was a success for him! It was not enough to keep him out of the courts, however, and the following year we find him sued for bankruptcy in Ipswich and Bristol.

George Stevens' roadside memorial in Southam [T.N. Curr]

The problem presented to the freeholders by trainers using the common was a constant source of friction during the nineteenth century. This new usage of the common had no legal precedent as a guide. Some freeholders entered into private arrangements with individual trainers under the threat of court action for following an activity which, in theory, could be considered as causing damage to the grazing. However, the main method seems to have been based on the freeholders, meeting as a vestry, entering into arrangements with individual trainers such as the three discussed above. This safeguarded the rights of all the commoners and provided some parish income – another angle on the familiar theme of the importance of the community over the individual.

The story of the races on Cleeve Hill has never been told before. This by itself justifies its inclusion in a history of the hill, but it bears a wider significance also. It marks the entry on to the hill of the influence of a wider, developing world in which wealth, leisure and recreation were playing an increasingly large part. It was a world in which the inhabitants of small villages like Bishop's Cleeve, Southam and Woodmancote could not, for the most part, hope to enter. It threatened their way of life, made them feel inferior and reinforced their need to knit together as a community in order to survive. The old division of Cleeve Common into its Bishop's Cleeve and Southam parcels ceased to have any meaning as past conflicts were forgotten in the face of the greater threat from outside. And yet the old continuities of grazing, quarrying and living on the hill remained.

FURTHER READING

The best account of the development of Cheltenham, without which this chapter, and following chapters, would make little sense is still Gwen Hart's *A History of Cheltenham* (Leicester University Press, Leicester, 1965, reprinted Alan Sutton Publishing, Gloucester, 1981). Steven Blake and Roger Beacham's *The Book of Cheltenham* (Barracuda Books, Buckingham, 1982) provides a more varied but briefer approach. Owen Ashton, 'Clerical Control and Radical Responses in Cheltenham Spa 1838–1848', *Midland History*, Volume 8, (1983), pages 121–47, sets the controversies over the races into the Cheltenham context.

The story of the races has been pieced together principally from the collection of local papers in Cheltenham Library – *Cheltenham Chronicle*, *Cheltenham Journal* (from 1824), *Cheltenham Free Press* (from 1834) and *Cheltenham Examiner* (from 1839). The main source for the career of George Stevens was *The Sporting Life*, copies of which are held in the British Newspaper Library at Colindale, North London. Also in Cheltenham Library are the Close controversy pamphlets and other miscellaneous ephemera related to the races.

The vestry minutes of Bishop's Cleeve which have provided the free-holders' perspective on the races are in the County Record Office, indexed under P46.

CHAPTER SIX

The Common Under Threat
(1818–1890)

Such a large space of common land, at such an elevation, and
within easy reach of the town, is a very great advantage.
S.S. Buckman, *Cheltenham as a Holiday Resort*, 1897

Sources and Contexts

We know so much about the commoners' reactions to Cheltenham races
because of the survival of such a good collection of parish records held in the
County Record Office in Gloucester. From these same records it is possible to
trace the more traditional uses of the common during the nineteenth century,
to learn more about the continuing demands of grazing, quarrying and
settlement which began to change the appearance of the hill in this period,
leaving many traces for the careful observer to seek out and identify.

The Industrial Revolution and the rapid growth of population, particularly in the developing industrial centres of the north and the Midlands, had
the effect of making traditional rural societies like Bishop's Cleeve and
Southam increasingly part of a pre-industrial past, despite their own
modest population growth. Evidence for this growth lies not in the fields on
the scarp slopes as in the Middle Ages, but in the growing number of houses
appearing on the hill at this time.

The Common as Grazing Ground

We have already read how for two or three days each year, for a total of
twenty-two years, the rights to grazing were literally overridden by outsiders from Cheltenham. What was happening during the rest of the year?

The enjoyment of grazing rights continued to be the greatest contribution
the common made to the local community, but the nature of the conflict of
interests over such rights now changed somewhat. The struggles between

119

the farmers of Bishop's Cleeve and Southam over their respective rights to common gave way to an informal system of management by the vestry meeting in Bishop's Cleeve and squabbles over boundary infringements became an activity of the past. The manorial boundary ceased to have any real significance. Although Lord Ellenborough had a new description of the boundary drawn up when he reinstituted beating the bounds of Southam manor in 1830, this archaic practice continued only until 1855 by which time the manor was ceasing to have any real significance. This was confirmed by the Ordnance Survey commissioners who had been given the task of drawing parish boundaries on their maps. As a result of their visits in 1880 and 1882 the whole of the common became part of Southam parish. By the deletion of a few lines on a map a link with the past and a source of much litigation and argument was ended by 'foreigners'. Yet again, the local inhabitants were subject to a decision taken elsewhere.

The major development of the common as grazing land during the nineteenth century concerned the first real attempts to control its over-use. In June 1821 the vestry meeting in Bishop's Cleeve took the important step of appointing a haywarden to enforce stinting, keep walls and hedges in good repair and impound all animals not marked as belonging to those local people who possessed rights to the common. The haywarden was then hired each year from May to September at a wage variously fixed at 5s. per week, or 16s. to £1 per month.

The post had varied success. Stinting still proved an elusive goal. In 1839 the Tithe Commissioners reported, 'There has in practice been no limit of common exercised over the common lands by the inhabitants', and ten years later Magdalen College, Oxford, which had an estate in Brockhampton, repeated the assertion. More was accomplished in the securing of the boundaries. In 1826 the freeholders paid to put all the walls and gates in good order; in 1835 part of the newly revived race fund was used to repair two gates; in 1836 and 1837 further repairs to gates and fences were authorized out of the same fund. Acting through the haywarden the vestry forced quarrymen to fence the quarries and claimed compensation for encroachments on to the common. In 1834 Thomas and James Simons were fined £2 to pay for a wall around their quarry, and a Mr Hill was ordered to fence his quarries otherwise compensation had to be paid. The lack of any further reference to the cases suggests the notices were obeyed. Finally, 'strangers'' animals disappeared off the common, easily identifiable because they lacked the mark applied by the haywarden for which 2d. per animal was added to his wage.

At last there was a system and mechanism for controlling the grazing on the common. Why had it taken until 1821 to introduce it? An answer to this question can only be found rooted in the contemporary attitudes which regarded all regulation with scepticism, even if the community's best interests were not being served by existing practices.

As the nineteenth century unfolded the necessity for regulation became more and more apparent, not just for the local inhabitants. A large number of them claimed right to the common. In 1695 we observed that eighty-five freeholders from Bishop's Cleeve prepared to defend their common grazing rights. An unknown, but obviously much smaller, number from Southam agreed to do the same. In 1847, when the open fields of the ancient parish were enclosed, 159 people made claim to Cleeve Common. The demands of traditional use on this valuable resource were still considerable, and the new demands issuing from Cheltenham increased the pressure. This was paralleled elsewhere, especially around London as explained in the Introduction. The 1845 General Enclosure Act had made it easier to enclose such land, to the detriment of the common grazing rights of farmers and labourers. Over 600,000 acres were enclosed during the following twenty-five years. In 1865 the Commons, Open Spaces and Footpaths Preservation Society was set up. The management of Cleeve Common towards the latter part of the nineteenth century can be viewed as a series of steps taken in an attempt to respond to pressures such as these. What were these steps?

In 1867 the freeholders met in Bishop's Cleeve church to set up a committee to enquire into the future uses of the common. It reported that the responsibility for fencing the quarries belonged to the lords of the manors, who owned the mineral rights; that the position of haywarden should be reinstated, having lapsed some time previously (an indication, perhaps, of a lessening of pressure for grazing as the population level stabilized and then fell in the middle years of the century). They also recommended that a subscription list should be opened to pay his wage, and other expenses. A rare statement of account survives from 1885. Receipts came from subscriptions (£8), from shepherding of the flocks (£18), and a fine from overstocking (£1). As the hayward received £30. 12s. 6d. for his work, the committee ended up in deficit in that year.

By this latter date the *ad hoc* committee was unable to deal with the pressures being placed upon the common, and the commoners took the decision to apply for the uses of the common to be regulated under the 1876 Commons Act. A provisional order was acquired but opposed by the local labourers because they feared for the loss of their rights of access. Pressure from outside, resulting from the desire of Cheltenham Corporation to safeguard access for its inhabitants, had split the local community into those in favour (landowners and farmers) and those against (labourers). As a result a parliamentary enquiry was held in Bishop's Cleeve in March and April 1890. Its minutes throw much contemporary light on the uses of the common, and attitudes to those uses.

We read of some familiar features; of upward of nine hundred sheep and two hundred cattle plus a small number of horses and donkeys pasturing on the thousand acres; of uncertain stinting arrangements; of stone quarried as

The conservators usually met at the Rising Sun. This photograph was taken in the garden during the 1930s [V. Gardner]

and when required; and of the failure of earlier attempts to reconcile the conflicts. We are also given different perspectives on familiar themes. Horse training disturbed the sheep, but the sheep sheltered behind the hurdles erected as practice jumps, and several had been killed when the horses landed. Individual commoners had extracted illegal payments from the horse trainers as a form of blackmail, as much as £25 in one case. Nobody called to give evidence could actually state what had happened to the money given to the earlier *ad hoc* vestry committee. There is a striking similarity in the evasiveness over answering such questions with the witnesses called in the Elizabethan court cases three centuries earlier.

The result of the enquiry was the passing on 4 July 1890 of the 'Commons Regulation (Cleeve) Provisional Order Confirmation Act'. It laid down the regulations under which the common is still run, the summary of which appears at the main entrances to the common. For £50 per annum Cheltenham bought the right of free access for its inhabitants for recreational use together with the right to elect three representatives to the Board of Conservators which was established to regulate and control all uses of the

The Washpool is no longer used for sheep-dipping, but its earlier importance can be seen in this photograph taken in the inter-war period [V. Gardner]

common. They were to be joined by three members from Bishop's Cleeve, two each from Woodmancote and Southam, and one representative of the lord of the manor of Bishop's Cleeve and of Southam.

The conservators were given wide powers. These included the power to fence quarries and plant trees to protect the animals; to permit the training of horses and the establishment of military camps and military exercises; to drain, level and manure the common to improve the pasture; to allow all local inhabitants right of free access for playing games and other 'reasonable recreation'; and the ability to draw up byelaws to improve their control. In a far-sighted clause they were also empowered to preserve all the ancient earthworks on the common – one of the earliest examples in the country of such protection (the Ancient Monuments Act had been passed only eight years earlier) but too late to save most of the hillfort from being quarried away from the front. They were to receive their income principally from Cheltenham Corporation's £50 each year and by issuing annual training permits for two guineas for each racehorse. Many commoners welcomed the order but several could only regret the sell-out of their ancient exclusive rights for £50, which gave nearly fifty thousand people the right to the common to exercise their troublesome dogs or chase the sheep across the downs. The locals' only tangible reward was the Washpool built in 1897 in Watery Bottom.

The act also laid down that animals could graze on the common from 25 April to 30 November each year and that the Board of Conservators should meet quarterly to discuss the management of the common. All activities on the common come under the jurisdiction of the conservators. Their establishment under the act of 1890 marked a turning-point in the history of the common. On the one hand it has ensured the continued use of the common as traditional grazing ground and went some way towards reconciling the conflicting uses demanded of it. On the other hand it marked the end of its traditional place in the economy and society of the villages lying at its feet. It became, legally, part of a wider context, as a recreational open space for Cheltenham and subject to national legislation. The nature of its function had changed and the animals on the common in the summer today, although important for their owners, are now a minor part of the life on the hill, no longer its chief reason for continuing to exist as common land. They remind us of a past age but are now peripheral to the common's main uses. The legislation of the year 1890 played an important part in laying the foundations of the modern perceptions of Cleeve and its common.

Quarrying

The existence of the quarries on Cleeve is a major feature of its landscape, particularly on the face around Cleeve Cloud, and yet their existence also yields little of their history. It has already been explained how their scale of operation was never large, and consequently few records still survive to allow a reconstruction of their development. However a body of documents does survive in the County Record Office which covers the three decades before 1850. From these documents the following tale can be told.

These three decades saw some of the busiest years for building in Cheltenham, and the demand for Cleeve Hill stone, although not so good in quality as that from Leckhampton, increased sufficiently to make quarrying a more attractive proposition, and a number of quarrymen took on the leases of various quarries which can be found in the Southam manor records. A survey of part of Southam manor taken in August 1829 suggests that there were only two areas of large scale quarrying on the hill, at Postlip and around Cleeve Cloud. Other records support this conclusion.

In December 1825 two Winchcombe men, William Powell, described as a quarryman, and Anthony Hampton, a wheelwright, took out a lease on a quarry near Cleeve Cloud. The terms provide a rare and interesting glimpse of the conditions of a quarrying lease:

The said William Powell and Anthony Hampton to work such quarry fair and not to do any wilful or unnecessary damage and to clear away all Rubbish and make good the Soil as they go, and so fence and guard such Quarry that nothing depasturing on the said Common can receive any Injury therefrom.

The Delaberes thus put their responsibility for fencing, as lords of the manor, on to their lessees. A clause in the lease forbidding haulage of stone along the Southam Road between October and February on pain of a £5 fine indicated the poor condition of the roads and the problems of haulage down off the hill at that time. By Lady Day 1831 the lessees were in arrears with their rent (to a sum of £67. 7s. 6d.) – a not uncommon state of affairs. William Powell seems also to have rented the Postlip quarries for at some time in the early 1830s (the actual date is unclear) we find that Henry Gaskins took over Powell's quarries at Postlip, which he then sublet.

Henry Gaskins' name appears most frequently in the court rolls as a lessee of the quarries. He built Laburnum Cottage, just above Spring Lane, on land stolen from the common, and was allowed to keep it because his quarry leases were a source of profit, first to the Delaberes and Coxwells, then to Lord Ellenborough. He seems to have taken his first lease in 1826, and paid £50 per annum for the quarries to at least 1842, when we find him having built a lime kiln and defaulted on the rent. Soon after that the quarry's lease passed to William Denley of Upper Bottomley and then to Thomas Yeend in October 1845 for £30 per annum. The importance of the quarries to the manors can be measured from two entries in the court rolls. In 1828 Gaskins was excused his rental because he was supplying the Coxwell manor with stone; in 1831 Lord Ellenborough also excused him his rental.

These quarries produced freestone of quality good enough for making ashlar blocks. Not all the stone was of such quality. Roadstone was taken from quarries on the top of the hill. In 1890 the enquiry into the common recorded the opening of a new quarry there, possibly Roadstone Quarry which today houses the equipment shed of the golf club. The enquiry also recorded the quarries were by then little used and the stone of poor quality, not worth taking three miles. Gravel continued to be extracted on a small scale from several places, such as that which led to the King's Beeches excavation in 1902. There is just one more reference to an identifiable quarry – that of Davis near Wheeler's quarry above Prestbury, which was paying a £6 rental when Lord Ellenborough bought the Delabere manor in 1831. It produced coarse stone for building foundations but cost 4d. or 5d. per cubic foot to extract, and sold for 3d. profit. It was said to have been open for four years, and worked by two men for a few weeks each winter. The profits were so low it was not worth extending it, although Wheeler's quarry, over the parish boundary, was obviously being worked at the time.

We know little of how the stone was used, particularly in Cheltenham. However, the details of the building of the former primary school in Bishop's Cleeve have survived, and from the rather confused accounts we can understand a little about using the stone. The school was built in 1845 by the National Schools' Society to replace the schoolroom above the porch. The stone came from Postlip Quarry and was rough cut to shape before being brought to the school site, where it was finished and stacked before being used. The accounts provide a further example of the problems of haulage which was one of the inhibiting features against large scale exploitation of the quarries. Five hundred cubic feet of good quality freestone cost £21. 10s. to purchase at the quarry, but £46 to haul down into Bishop's Cleeve. The building of the new school exemplified the problems which have faced the exploitation of the quarries throughout our story.

Woodland

By the early nineteenth century a pattern of woodland had been established which has remained largely intact until today, although the modern neglect of woodland has destroyed the regular coppicing of the scarp woods, and many timber trees have fallen through decay and have not been felled for use. However, with the exception of the wood at Wontley discussed in the next section, the extent of the woodland has changed little in the past two centuries.

Ring dating of ash trees felled on the lower edge of Stutfield Wood suggests they were planted or emerged as seedlings about 1830, the time when Lord Ellenborough was buying the Southam manors. We know that he considered the valuation of the timber on the Coxwell part of the manor too high at £2,176, but this included trees in hedges and along the roadsides in addition to Stutfield, Thrift and Queen's Woods. As with the story of the common as grazing ground, the woodland can be left at the end of the nineteenth century in the knowledge that the twentieth century has not brought any major change to its form, but has brought decline to its traditional use and value.

Settlement

The main feature of changes in settlement during this period was the continuing encroachment around the edges of the common by families stealing a small piece of land and settling there. The 1847 Enclosure Map shows the situation in mid-century. Mention has been made earlier of how the Kitchen family had taken in land from the common by 1793 (plot

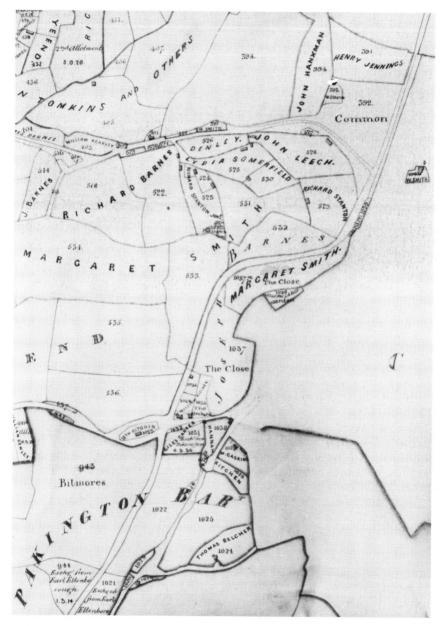

Bishop's Cleeve Enclosure Map of 1847 clearly shows encroachments along the lanes and on to the common [Gloucestershire Record Office]

Horses Green in Stockwell Lane – a reminder of a roadside encroachment

1030); how Henry Gaskins had been allowed to retain his enclosure (1029); of Captain Barnett's training stables (1040); and how in 1866 George Stevens purchased a cottage built on land taken from the common before 1716 (528).

Encroachments alongside the lanes leading to the hill, particularly Stockwell Lane, continued and were consolidated. The narrow plots on the northern side of Richard Barnes' fields (518, 522) show this process under way. The house on one of these plots carries the name Horses Green to remind the passer-by that two centuries or more ago this lane was wider and flanked by wide verges where animals could graze. This process can also be observed along the earlier turnpike route across the hill, particularly where it passed through plots 1022 and 1025. Here the chief transgressor can clearly be identified as Thomas Belcher (1024).

The whole of the adjoining area, as indicated by its name, Hillground, had at some earlier date been stolen from the common. By 1800 or soon after Thomas and his wife were working a small quarry there. By 1833 they had built a house and outbuildings at the rather large cost of £210. He actively added to his land by encroachment, and in the Southam manor court of 1855 he was accused of encroaching 4 ft on to the old road, and ordered to demolish his wall. He obviously refused because he was

The addition of landowners' names to the Enclosure Map clearly illustrates the large number of smaller landowners in Bishop's Cleeve compared to the domination of Lord Ellenborough in Southam. This pattern had been established by the later Middle Ages [Gloucestershire Record Office]

presented for the same offence again in 1861 – presumably with the same results for Spring Lane today becomes a very narrow footpath. Even the tighter manorial control in Southam in the mid-nineteenth century lacked the real power to reassert community interest over the interests of the individual. The decisions by Lord Ellenborough's court to receive rents from the Kitchens, Gaskins and also the Hawkers at Nutterswood rather than evict them, is clear evidence of this change in attitude.

Such examples show how difficult it proved to control what is traditionally known as squatters' settlement, even where tight manorial control lasted into the relatively late date of the second half of the nineteenth century. This is apparent in the Enclosure Map from the pattern of land-owning. Note how the northern (upper) part in Bishop's Cleeve has many names placed across the fields signifying a fragmented pattern of landownership with many encroachments, while the lower part is dominated by Lord Ellenborough and has few encroachments, especially away from the common.

The boundary between the manors is shown by a dark line. The original map in the County Record Office is shaded blue and red, and this boundary is much clearer. It is uncertain where it runs along Rising Sun Lane; not until the Ordnance Survey commissioners arrived in 1880 was this part clearly defined. By building exactly on the line of the boundary families could claim to have built in the other manor. Hannah Kitchen managed to avoid paying rental to Southam manor till 1834 when her claim that she lived in Bishop's Cleeve was finally rejected. It was not difficult to identify continued encroachment on this map from the deeds dated 1866. The yard and stable (now Sunnyside) had been added to the original encroachment.

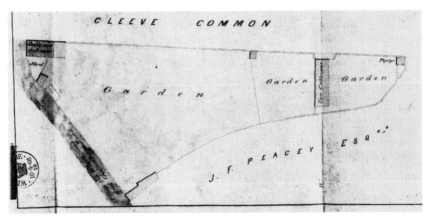

This map taken from the Kitchen family deeds shows how the cottage now called Sunnyside (top left) was built on an encroachment into the common at the top of Stockwell Lane [R. Salter]

A little below them, newly built by 1847, lay the Tower House, home of Giles Carter, a professional man whose Gothic folly would seem to be the first house built on the hill for somebody who was not economically dependant upon its resources. A variety of myths surround the house, but the fact is that it was built straddling the manorial boundary. In 1855 the perambulators of the boundary kept to their route by forcing a window to follow the boundary through the house. He was away when this happened, and his reaction is not recorded!

This, then, was the nature of the community on Cleeve Hill right up to the last decade of the nineteenth century. It comprised a small population mostly made up of the families of quarrymen and hauliers, stonemasons, and stonecutters. Only the Rising Sun stood as a exception to this localized economy, taking its living from passing trade. It had developed as a hotel where the summit of the road of 1823 crossed Gambles Lane as it led on to the common from the vale.

The houses of this period are still recognizable today. They were originally unpretentious, rather low Cotswold stone houses, devoid, with the notable exception of the Tower, of any embellishments. They appear as evidence of the period when Cleeve Hill and its common still held economic importance for a small number of people on the periphery of the parish.

A Boxing Day meet at the Rising Sun in the first decade of the twentieth century [T.N. Curr]

None of the people were farmers, for the poor quality land in small fields could not, by themselves, sustain a farm. The possible exception was Longwood Farm on Nottingham Hill, dating from at least before 1779 when Samuel Rudder, in his county history, recorded that the proprietor was prospecting for coal on his land. In searching for the farmers we must now return to Wontley, Cockbury and Haymes as the former fields of the medieval settlements continued to bring hope and despair to successive occupiers and owners.

The fields of Wontley continued to belong to the Lawrence family of Sandywell Park. In 1828 West Wood and Wontley Wood were purchased by John Prince for £3,500. Yet again another owner hit hard times. This led to the clearance of Wontley Wood and some replanting in order to raise capital, but unsuccessfully, and in 1833 he sold the holding to Walter Lawrence for only £3,000. After around one thousand years, therefore, an ancient boundary lost meaning as land attached to Wontley farm now straddled it, although it continues as a parish boundary to the present day, and the former outline of Wontley Wood can still be recognized in the field boundaries. The arable acreage thus grew to 320, which were leased later in 1833 to John and George Lane for ten years at £150 annual rental, together with thirty-four acres of West Wood for £25. The 1841 Tithe Map recorded the nature of the farm at Wontley; 236 acres of arable; 88 acres of pasture; and 66 acres of West Wood reserved to Walter Lawrance. The 1851 census recorded three small households at Wontley, of an agricultural labourer, a shepherd and a farmer. With the clearance of the woodland in the early 1830s Wontley took on much of its present appearance. Modern farming techniques enable profitable crops to be grown and the area of arable is probably similar to that of the medieval village. The lack of a farmhouse, however, is a reminder in the landscape of the broken hearts and pockets of those who sought, and failed, to make a living from this deserted spot on the far side of the common.

Cockbury fared better. It remained a tenanted farm, with a mixed economy. The Tithe Map recorded 140 acres in Bishop's Cleeve parish farmed by George Hone, who, unlike the tenants at Wontley, played a prominent part in parish affairs during this period. The fields have retained this mixed use down to the present. They can be observed from the Cheltenham to Winchcombe road, but the farm buildings have been converted to holiday cottages – a late-twentieth-century reminder that Cleeve Hill can still lay claim to being a holiday resort.

The appearance of Haymes has been transformed during the past twenty years by the building of a mushroom farm. This provides the greater part of the income of the estate which is now much smaller than at any time in the past. William Strachan's house has been largely demolished to leave one wing remaining. As at Cockbury the twentieth century has been one of the periods of greatest change in its recorded history.

Looking across the Longcroft to Haymes before the building of the mushroom farm in the 1960s

Recreation

At first glance it might seem unnecessary to include here a section on recreation, having taken a whole chapter to investigate Cheltenham races on Cleeve Hill, but those were not the only recreational activities taking place in the nineteenth century. From the evidence to the select committee which led to the act of 1890, people from Cheltenham came to the hill for football, cricket and other games in addition to walking across the common for enjoyment of the open space. We have no record of how many people or how often they came, except it was too often for the commoners. However, we do have evidence for one particular type of visitor, which provides the focus of this section.

In July 1846 a small number of county gentry, clergy and would-be gentry met together to establish a society with the aim of 'seeking Nature in her remoter haunts', five or six times a year. Thus was born the Cotteswold Naturalists' Field Club. Inevitably one of the remoter haunts was Cleeve and their minutes record several visits to the common between 1846 and the end of the century. In 1852 and 1857 they visited Postlip and Cleeve Cloud Quarries respectively in a search for fossils. At the latter date part of the membership went searching for butterflies over at Postlip. In May 1859 another visit started with breakfast at The Lamb in Cheltenham's High

Street, then by omnibus to the foot of Cleeve from where the geologists walked to Rolling Bank Quarry. We find in the society's minutes further interesting detail on quarrying, for in 1859 Rolling Bank had been newly opened; the members returned again in 1863 and 1865 at which latter date they examined a tunnel from which stone had been extracted and stacked up – rare reference to mining which was so important in the Southern Cotswolds near Bath.

Another similar county society, the Bristol and Gloucestershire Archaeological Society, was founded in 1876. It attracted the same type of membership as the Field Club. The minutes of their meetings record only one visit to the hill during the period covered by this chapter. In summer 1889 over a hundred members and friends visited Cleeve Camp on their way to Winchcombe, Spoonley Roman Villa and Whittington Court. The foremost county archaeologist of the day, G.F. Witts, addressed the party on the latest thinking on the nature of the camp.

Such visitors were learned, serious-minded and aware of their position as visitors to a valuable economic resource. They contrasted starkly with the more usual visitor seeking an open space for fun and games. The new conflict that this brought, which first emerged during the years studied in this chapter, was only partly resolved by the passing of the regulation act of 1890. This new leisure-orientated conflict replaced the older ones over manorial rights and land use which provided the driving force throughout most of the hill's history. The final two chapters investigate the attempts to balance such conflicting demands during the twentieth century.

FURTHER READING

The secondary sources detailed at the end of the last chapter provide the general background to this chapter also. Most of the primary sources have been consulted in the County Record Office. These include Bishop's Cleeve vestry minutes, tithe and enclosure awards (P46 collection). Further details of the 1847 enclosure are catalogued under D2216. Southam manor records in D2025, Boxes 31/69/70 contained material on the quarries. Bishop's Cleeve school details were found in D2186/13; and Wontley details in D444 collection. The Ordnance Survey boundary books were consulted at their headquarters in Southampton; the parliamentary enquiry minutes at the House of Lords – (*Report from the Select Committee on Commons; together with the proceedings of the committee and minutes of evidence* dated 17 April 1890). The proceedings and transactions of the two county societies can be consulted in Cheltenham or Gloucester libraries. Copies of the decennial census since 1841 are available in Gloucester Library, which also keeps a register of the locations in the county where the large scale Ordnance Survey maps can be consulted.

CHAPTER SEVEN

The 'Cotswold Health Resort' (1890–1914)

Cleeve 'Ill is a town consisting of several bungalows, one hotel, one stables, two hundred and forty-three stone walls, one golf links, one post-office, one hill, and a large number of other useful institutions, such as a tin church, a sanitory, and a tramline.
Selina Jenkins' Letter, *Cheltenham Chronicle and Gloucester Graphic*,
18 April 1903

Context and Perceptions

Most people who come to Cleeve Hill reach it along the Cheltenham to Winchcombe road. It is certainly no ordinary Cotswold village, and even if it no longer quite corresponds to the fictitious Selina Jenkins' satirical description at the turn of the century, it is still recognizably the same place. This chapter tells the story of the great changes which took place in the three decades before the outbreak of the First World War, transforming the small, rather poor hamlet towards the peripheries of the parish of Bishop's Cleeve into an affluent suburb and favourite day-trip resort for the people of Cheltenham and further afield. In these three decades the hill experienced its greatest changes since at least the creation of its modern agrarian landscape at the end of the Middle Ages or even, arguably, since the original clearances before and during the Bronze Age. Why did they happen then?

The growing use of the common as Cheltenham's 'lung' was explored in the previous chapter. Cleeve Hill was readily accessible, even on foot, to the people of the expanding town, but as improvements in transport occurred, then accessibility improved and this enticed more people to enjoy the air and the privileges brought under the 1890 Act. From September 1891 horse-drawn buses ran to Southam; three years later they climbed to the Rising Sun; in August 1901 electric tramcars started to run to the Malvern View. According to the *Cheltenham Examiner*, ten thousand passengers were

135

CHELTENHAM CHRONICLE AND GLOUCESTERSHIRE G

WINCHCOMBE DAME *(who has got as far as Cleeve Hill for the first time since the tramway was commenced)*: Lawks-a-mussey; what be they posts and wire for, Jaarge?

HER HUSBAND: The 'lectric tramway, o' coorse! The papers calls it "the overhead trolley" — zummat.

WINCHCOMBE DAME: Well, if they runs trollers on they wires, I doon't wonder they overturns, and I'm afeared the lighter cars they talks aboot woont be mooch beeter.

LADY'S MIDNIGHT ADVENTURE.   OUR DEFECTIVE RIFLES.

An old attitude in a new guise — the contrast between the sophistication of Cheltenham and the rusticity of the local inhabitants is clearly reflected in this cartoon concerning the arrival of the tramway on Cleeve Hill. The reference is to the fatal crash on one of the test runs in July 1901 [Cheltenham Library]

carried on the first Sunday of operation. Taken literally, a fifth of the population of Cheltenham moved out of town for the day.

The context of life on Cleeve Hill was increasingly 'Cheltenhamized'. Not only did a large number of Cheltenham traders and merchants come to live on the hill with their families, but also a vast amount of Cheltenham capital was invested in the rapidly growing settlement. At all periods the importation of 'foreign' capital has been a powerful force for change.

Cleeve Hill became a fashionable place to live for affluent people, ironically, seeking peace and quiet after a hectic day in the town. Many owned their own houses; others took long-term lets. The 'trippers' who followed took short lets and day trips. They each had their own perceptions of the place. Even today the visitor cannot fail to notice the comfortable living still evidenced by the turn-of-the-century mansions, expressions of the wealth and self-confidence of self-made men looking down on humanity,

The tramstop outside the Malvern View shortly after opening. The view also shows Henry Norton's pine villa Fernclyffe on the left, and Arthur Yiend's cart on the right

not now from the ramparts of the Iron Age hillfort, but from the wooden balconies of pine villas. They shared with the day tripper the desire to escape to the common, to breathe the air, to walk the downs. And, even if they played golf while the latter played football, they shared the view that the commoners' animals were mere nuisances intruding into 'their' landscape.

Wealth, however, did bring privileges not available to the day tripper. Private transport if the tram was crowded; tea on their own lawn rather than in a crowded tea garden; comfortable rooms rather than cramped lodgings as demand outstripped supply. Selina Jenkins recorded how she was given a room which could only be reached through the bedroom of another guest. She also remarked on the discarded orange peel, broken ginger beer bottles and used tram tickets which littered the roadside. Clearly the 'Cotswold Health Resort' had different perceptions for the different people intent on enjoying its life and facilities. When the desirability of the tramway was debated in Cheltenham's council-chamber in 1898, the golfers and the trainers, themselves comparative newcomers, condemned the proposal. It would bring 'the scum of the earth' to strew empty beer bottles around. They were just two more groups trying to protect their own self-interest against outside intrusions. Like the others, they failed. A month

The Cleeve Hill café could cater for parties of 200 'at the shortest notice'. Built in 1901, it was let to Ernest Batstone of Bath Road – another example of Cheltenham initiatives and capital exploiting the potential of the hill

The Geisha Tea House offered full board from Saturday evening to Monday morning for 10s. 6d. in 1909. It stood just above the tramstop

before the trams arrived in July 1901, the *Cheltenham Chronicle and Gloucester Graphic* described the resort in these terms:

> ... and every little shed and shanty has invested in a pennyworth of cardboard, on which the classic legends 'Tea and Hot water', 'Aerated Waters', 'Furnished Apartments', and so forth are inscribed in fearful and wonderful characters to entice the simple trammist. Enormous trades-men's mansions erect their ponderous walls on the hill slope, bungalows spring up in every corner like mustard and cress, the most improbable sites are staked out and divided into streets and alleys by the prospective builder, the land goes up in price 500 per cent.

The vitality and excitement of these years comes across well, but why so much interest then? In searching for an answer to this question, it is necessary first to examine how the hill came to be associated with healthy living.

The Cotswold Convalescent Home

The story originates in Cheltenham. On 25 May 1892 a small group of public-spirited townspeople met in the Victoria Home in St James' Square to establish a convalescent home as a charity for inhabitants of Cheltenham recovering from free hospital treatment but without the means, financial or

The Convalescent Home shortly before the First World War

domestic, for a period of convalescence. A subscription list was opened; a site investigated; and enquiries made of suitable builders. With speed difficult to understand today, within two months £600 had been raised by subscription, a further £100 promised and a gift of £1,200 made available. The committee therefore were able to accept a tender of £1,284 from Messrs. Billings to build the home. By the following March, the building was well under way. The site chosen was a disused quarry by the main road on Cleeve Hill, at a cost of £150. The only reason for the choice seemed to be that it was available at a satisfactory price. Would the subsequent history of Cleeve Hill have been the same if it had been built elsewhere, perhaps on Leckhampton Hill?

The home was formally opened by the local MP Sir John Dorington on the second Saturday of July, less than fourteen months after the initial decision to build had been taken. The home catered for six men and six women during the summer months from April to the end of October. Then it closed for the winter because it was felt the cost of running the home in the cold months would be too great. Ninety-nine patients stayed during the four months of its first season. Welcome as any period of convalescence must have been to its patients, the regime prompts comparison with that threat to all working-class aspiration and endeavour – the Union Work-house. This is well illustrated by the house rules:

Morning prayers	8.15
Breakfast	8.30
Dinner	12.30
Tea	4.30
Supper	8.00
Prayers	9.00

– No going home without leave.
– No visiting public or other houses without permission.
– Males and females must not talk to each other or walk with each other. They must keep to their own side of the grounds.

The parallel with the workhouse can be developed. The first concerns of the Poor Law Guardians were the ratepayers, not the workhouse inmates. The highlight of the year at the home was the annual subscribers' tea, held in the summer on the lawn. It followed a brief inspection and even briefer formal meeting (fifteen minutes long in 1895). It was a large affair, attended by a hundred subscribers and guests, headed by the mayor. There could have been no greater symbol of the influence of Cheltenham. From the poorest to the most affluent, the townspeople claimed Cleeve as their own, at least until 1899 when the subscribers' tea began to be taken in Cheltenham.

Yet we must not dismiss unfairly the efforts of late-Victorian philanthropy. Within two years four more beds had been established to meet the obvious need for the home, and the idea was only kept alive by generous giving. The annual subscription of a guinea gave the right to nominate one person for a two week stay for a maximum charge of 5s. per week. As the home had a close connection with Cheltenham General Hospital, many patients were able to stay at no cost to themselves at all.

These arrangements for the running of the home lasted until the First World War. From 1902 it remained open until the end of November and in 1909 the building was extended as the result of an appeal in memory of H.T. Carrington, who had been treasurer and secretary for many years. Then, on the outbreak of war in 1914 the committee briefly offered the home to the War Office, before changing their mind and offering it to the Red Cross, who immediately sent to it sixteen wounded Belgian soldiers, in November 1914. It was run as part of the Red Cross hospital at New Court in Lansdown Road. For the first time in its history, there was no winter closure. Miss Eleanor Adlard of Postlip had already offered £25 to keep it open in the winter. She then provided the Christmas meal. During 1915, 217 British soldiers, 17 Belgian soldiers, 4 sailors and 33 civilians spent time at the home. The latter were still nominated by the subscribers; the rest paid for by the Red Cross. In 1916 the war came closer; the windows were blacked out and an insurance against air-raids taken; the paddock was dug up for potatoes. When the military finally left in January 1919 the home closed until April, as usual. On reopening, the charge had increased to 10s. per week, which was deeply regretted but unavoidable after the wartime inflation.

Cleeve Hill can still lay claim to being a health resort: a recent advertisement from the local newspaper [*Gloucestershire Echo*]

In 1923 it was bought by Courtaulds who enlarged it further by the addition of two glass and concrete wings. Since 1979 it has been a private nursing home, still fulfilling a function similar to its original purpose. It has therefore provided a thread of continuity throughout the twentieth century, but its nineteenth-century significance lay in the association it made between Cleeve Hill and health. It was the best advert any publicist could hope to discover. The Cotswold Convalescent Home rapidly became a catalyst for change.

Building the Health Resort

Of all the periods which have left their mark on the hill, that of the Cotswold Health Resort is probably the most obvious and the easiest for the visitors of today to discover and interpret for themselves. This part of the story of the landscape is the easiest to see; it is one of the most difficult to disentangle from the mass of written evidence which survives.

Our starting point must be the three Ordnance Survey maps shown here. The 1884 map recorded a community very similar in size and nature to that analysed for 1841. By 1923 the modern shape of the community on Cleeve Hill had been formed; development since then has reinforced the pattern

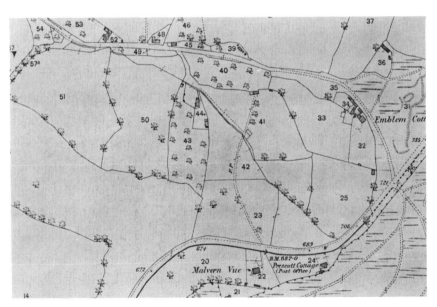

Cleeve Hill in 1884 [Reproduced from the Ordnance Survey 6 in map with the permission of the Controller of Her Majesty's Stationery Office © Crown copyright]

which had largely been established by 1914. This is the purpose of this section, to outline the processes of change which have so clearly left their mark in today's buildings.

The key to the development was improved transport, which enabled a variety of people to perceive the opportunity to make money by building on land bordering the main road, particularly the narrow strip lying between it and the earlier turnpike road. Most of the houses were built as speculation, financed by capital from the purses of wealthy Cheltenham entrepreneurs. Cleeve Hill became integrated into Cheltenham in both visible and invisible ways.

The development of the Cotswold Health Resort may be traced from two main sources: Kelly's directories, and the records of local estate agents Bayleys, who seemed to have possessed a near monopoly of the house and land transactions on the hill at this time. Neither source is without its problems. Kelly's continued to include outdated information. In 1863 it still carried the statement that Cheltenham races were held on Cleeve, eight years after the final unsuccessful attempt to restart them after a gap of thirteen years. However, the inclusion of Cleeve Hill as a separate entry in 1894 did mark a recognition of the growing separateness of the embryonic resort, now becoming noticeably different from the rural nature of Woodmancote with which it had previously been linked.

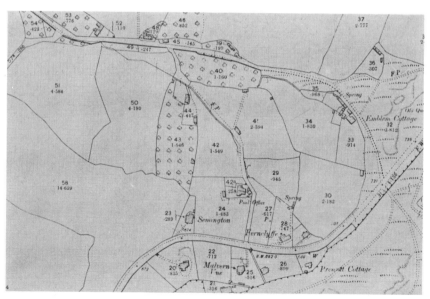

Cleeve Hill in 1902 [Reproduced from the Ordnance Survey 6 in map with the permission of the Controller of Her Majesty's Stationery Office © Crown copyright]

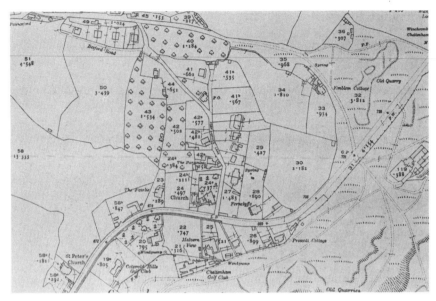

Cleeve Hill in 1923 [Reproduced from the Ordnance Survey 6 in map with the permission of the Controller of Her Majesty's Stationery Office © Crown copyright]

The difficulties with the Bayley's records lie in the identification of the separate houses and building plots. Geographical descriptions are imprecise, but more importantly the rapid turnover of residents led to frequent renaming of properties and consequent problems of continued identification. This can only really be done when other sources, particularly deeds, can be consulted. The house called Adderstone House, which stands at the bottom of Rising Sun Lane, has been altered several times in its history. It has also been called by a variety of different names. By 1872 it was called The Rockery, by 1897 it had been renamed Upmeads, by 1918 Petra, and by 1924 Heron Rock. In 1926 the name changed to Adderstone and, finally, to Adderstone House in 1966. This is an extreme case but illustrates well a major feature of the new settlement – the transient nature, not only of residents, but also of owners of properties. Emblem Cottage has retained its distinctive name since George Stevens' ownership, but after his son sold it in 1888 it had changed hands a further five times before being sold, in 1916, to a Mrs Pease, the wife of a colonel in the Indian Veterinary Department. Only one of these owners actually lived at Emblem Cottage. George Yiend, quarryman, bought it for £400 as the sitting tenant in 1888 but had to sell in 1897, being unable to pay off his mortgage. The history of Emblem Cottage

The side of Adderstone House quite clearly shows different phases of building to complement its frequent change of name. The architecture of the laundry, which served for a short time as St Peter's Church, still betrays this former use

well illustrates how the ownership of the existing buildings in 1884 moved from local people, as identified from the 1841 Tithe Map, to the wealthy of Cheltenham.

But the existing houses were insufficient for the demand. It is impossible to trace here the building of all the houses which appear on the later Ordnance Survey maps, but an indication of the process can be given in outline. The Malvern View was actually being built at the time of the 1881 census in March. Its neighbour Prescott Cottage has a stone dated four years earlier. Ashleigh, lower down the hill in Ashleigh Lane towards Cheltenham, was newly built in 1886. Upper Colletts (Plot 20 on the map of 1902; see page 143) was built a decade later for a local magistrate C.C. Turnbull of College Lawn, as a holiday residence and for letting. One local person who did enter into this housing speculation was George Yiend who lived in Laburnum Cottage on the common. He had Laburnum Villa built in his garden as a letting property. In 1900 it was let for £35 per annum. The architectural difference between the labourer's cottage and the speculative mansion is still very evident today despite more recent alterations. All these houses were built out of Cotswold stone, a tradition which was carried on late into the twentieth century. Fourwinds opposite the Cotswold Convalescent Home is said to have been the last property to have had local stone used on its construction, in an extension built shortly before the Second World War.

The similarity of style and stonework of many Cotswold stone houses betrays their common origin. They were built by Arthur Yiend: a local man of many interests who can most be considered responsible for the growth of the present village. He was most active in the two decades before he retired in 1920. He laid out Post Office Lane, where he lived at Denewood, which is marked as the Post Office on the 1902 map. In 1912 he extended the lane into Besford Road, which he constructed at the same time as he was providing the stone for Besford Court, near Pershore – hence the name. He built for sale and for rent, and although he was a local man, his money still came from Cheltenham in the form of mortgages. In comparison, Cheltenham builder Amos Wilson built only to clients' specifications. His work can be seen at its best at the bottom of the hill in the houses along Haymes Road. They could belong to any affluent suburb of the period.

The distinctive appearance of the hill itself as a health resort did not, however, depend upon Arthur Yiend's houses, for in their stone construction they shared a continuity with the past. The impression is rather to be found in the prefabricated, pine villas which were constructed at the very end of the nineteenth century. The first to appear were erected by T.W. Stephens, who

The style of the houses in Besford Road indicate they were built by Arthur Yiend. There are many other examples on the hill [T.N. Curr]

had a picture frame making establishment in Winchcombe Street in Cheltenham. He put two quite literally in the front garden of his own home, Ivybank in Lye Lane, for holiday letting in 1897. Two years later Walter Dicks, who owned a large soft furnishing emporium in the Lower High Street, had a much larger pine house erected on part of a plot he had recently purchased. He named it Semington. Today it is known as Wendlesclif. Three more similar houses soon followed. Fernclyffe became the home of Henry Norton, who owned an ironmongers which later became a motor depot on the corner of the Bath Road and the Strand. Greenmount was built in the grounds of The Malvern View for holiday letting by H.G. Swift. The fourth example was Hillview next to Prescott Cottage. These houses still help to give the hill its atmosphere of a holiday resort.

The division of the fields into building plots can also be traced in Bayley's records. The earliest reference to such plots in their records can be found in 1896, when half an acre near the Rising Sun went on the market for a hundred guineas freehold. The land market speeded up on the arrival of the tramway in 1901, as the map of Prescott Cottage on page 149 shows, but there is little evidence to support the claim in the *Cheltenham Chronicle* that land prices rose by 500 per cent, certainly not in the long term. Building plots costing £300 in 1896 were similarly priced in 1903, but rather easier to sell.

This page from Burrow's 1909 guide book to Cleeve Hill illustrates well some aspects of the developing health resort [Gloucester Library]

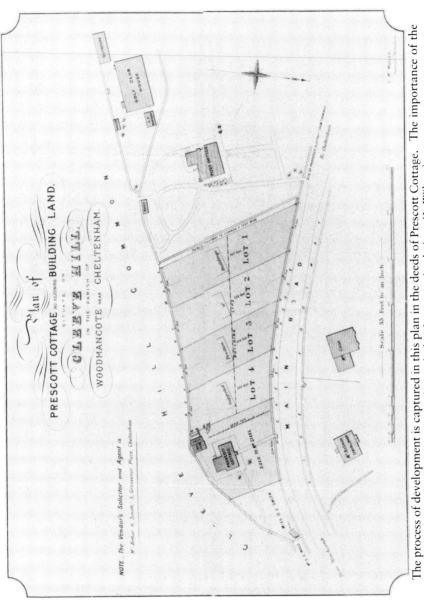

The process of development is captured in this plan in the deeds of Prescott Cottage. The importance of the tramway for such developments is obvious [J. Wilson]

Walter Dicks' pine villa Semington, now called Wendlescliff. The weather vane gives a clear clue to the date of construction

We must not, however, think that every venture was successful as far as the speculators were concerned. The best example of this was that part of the Wickfields lying opposite what is now the High Roost. In 1896 eight acres were purchased by C.B. Dix. He not only ran a builders' merchants and ironmongers in the Bath Road but was also landlord of many houses in that area of the town. He bought them for £500. Shortly afterwards he put the land back on the market as four building plots at £150 each plus six acres at £150 per acre. His profit would have been twice the purchase price. There were no takers and when the venture was repeated in 1903 it again failed. Today's visitor is perhaps thankful that not all speculation succeeded.

By 1914 the nature of the present village of Cleeve Hill had been established. Within a few years it had become an affluent outer suburb of Cheltenham and a holiday resort. It was publicized by an enormous variety of picture postcards and, from 1909, a series of guidebooks. They capture for us the spirit of the age and provide important clues for the reconstruction of the period. We have already remarked how many of the residents on the hill had businesses down in Cheltenham. They tended to move in to enjoy the wealth they had created, moving out when advancing years or, ironically, ill-health forced them into more accessible locations. None stayed for many years – it was a transient population, but at various times it included some of the well-known Cheltenham shopkeepers of the period: J.J. Banks the bookseller who lived at The Shanty and published *From a Cotswold Height*; Thomas George, bootmaker, who lived at Greenmount; J.S. Friskney who had a toyshop in Pittville Street and lived at Thrift Cottage; and Thomas Malvern, architect and surveyor, of Ivydene. They made their money in Cheltenham and enjoyed looking down on it. Butchers and bakers fell over themselves to make life on the hill as comfortable as possible. By 1911 the residents were well served by frequent visits on rounds from Cheltenham: butchers Holliday and Page even offered to send urgent orders by tram!

In the same way that the commoners of Bishop's Cleeve, Southam and Woodmancote found their traditional claims to the common being swamped by the trippers from Cheltenham demanding open space for their recreation, so the few families who had made a traditional living from the hill found themselves swamped by the newcomers. The main feature of this new life on the hill was its transience. As if to compensate for this, the

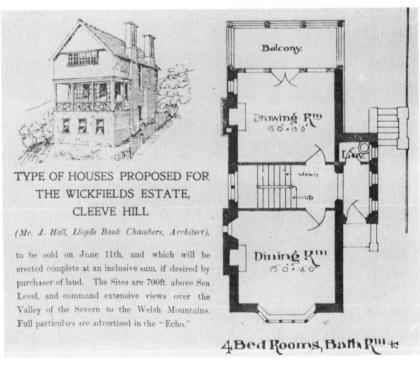

TYPE OF HOUSES PROPOSED FOR
THE WICKFIELDS ESTATE,
CLEEVE HILL

(Mr. J. Hall, Lloyds Bank Chambers, Architect).

to be sold on June 11th, and which will be erected complete at an inclusive sum, if desired by purchaser of land. The Sites are 700ft. above Sea Level, and command extensive views over the Valley of the Severn to the Welsh Mountains. Full particulars are advertised in the "Echo."

An advertisement for the failed Wickfields estate venture [Cheltenham Library] newcomers made attempts to establish institutions which would bind the community together and create for it an identity independent of the individuals who might at any one time belong to it; they met with varying success.

The Institutions of the Health Resort

Selina Jenkins noticed three institutions in her supposed visit in 1903. The 'sanitory' and tramline have already been discussed; the third was the tin church. The type of people who came to live on the hill were the backbone of many a church and chapel at the turn of the century, and their most earnest efforts went into the founding and upkeep of places of worship.

There was no place of worship on the hill till *c.* 1870 when Henry Taylor, an Anglican clergyman originally from London, converted the laundry behind his house in Rising Sun Lane into a chapel. Today, the Gothic architecture and iron cross are reminders of this former use. In 1896 he left,

NEW HOUSES ON CLEEVE HILL.
Cleeve Hill has become quite a popular residential resort, and some very nice new houses have been built there. The picture shows two just erected at Nutters' Wood, and which contain every convenience. The one on the left is to let. Mr. W. H. Horsley, of 9 Promenade, Cheltenham, will give particulars. A testimony to the healthiness of the site is furnished by the fact that the man (Thomas Yiend) shown at the top left of the picture has lived on Cleeve Hill 33 years, and the man (Eli Hawker) at the foot at Nutters' Wood 68 years. These new houses, as already indicated, occupy a unique and healthy position 800ft. above sea level, and are sheltered from the north, east, and north-east winds, and command magnificent views. There are three approaches, the nearest being that from Southam tram terminus. Mr. T. Malvern, architect.

A suburban villa at Nutterswood, advertised as newly built in 1908. Note the architect, Thomas Malvern, who himself lived on the hill [T.N. Curr]

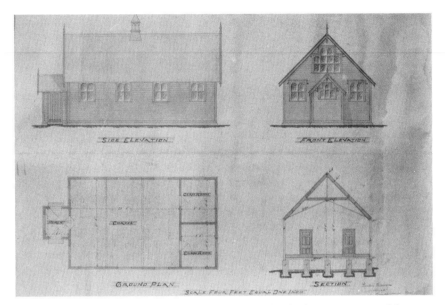

SIDE ELEVATION   *FRONT ELEVATION*

GROUND PLAN   *SECTION*

SCALE FOUR FEET EQUAL ONE INCH

A design for the Interdenominational Church which was unsuccessful

putting his house to rent. The services were stopped and for a time the worshippers shared in the morning services conducted in the Convalescent Home by Revd Thomas Jesson from Bishop's Cleeve. This did not meet their demand in the winter months when the home was closed and so in an attempt to establish a permanent place for worship, Mr and Mrs Thomas Astman made their home, Spring Bank, available for a Sunday School and an evening service between June and November 1900. Then Walter Dicks of Semington offered his stable loft for the winter months, but the congregations had grown so large that it was decided to build a proper church. On 26 June 1901 the Cleeve Hill Interdenominational Church was opened by Sir John Dorington.

It had an interesting mixture of Anglican and Nonconformist services; the former on Sunday morning, the latter in the evening, thereby catering for all people, who on their own could not sustain any one type of church. From the start the local traders played a large part. Walter Dicks gave the land at the cost price of £50; Arthur Yiend likewise built the foundations for £65; and the whole congregation contributed the £250 paid to the firm of James Lee of Manchester who won the contract to build the church with a lightweight patent design necessary because of the potential instability of the site.

An invitation to the first anniversary of the Interdenominational Church, before the church had its own pastor [J. Yiend]

The affluence of the congregation meant that finance was never a great problem, but the money had been made in the first place by people who knew what they wanted, and there was much wrangling and argument in the early years over such matters as who should play the organ or take the various Sunday School classes. Their first pastor, the Revd William Edwin Lewis from Leicester, took up his post in October 1909 after two others had turned it down. When he left in 1913 six ministers refused the living before a successor was found. It was not an easy congregation to minister to, but clearly a need was served. Over a hundred people regularly attended the annual teas held on the lawn of Fernclyffe, and before the First World War the Sunday School numbered over fifty scholars.

For the first eight years of its life the church had no resident pastor. That W.E. Lewis was appointed in 1909 was the result of two factors: one internal to the church, the second external. The first concerned the arrival on the hill in 1904 of General and Mrs Richard Oldfield, late of the Indian Army. Mrs Oldfield soon became superintendent of the Sunday School; her husband preferred to contribute in less obvious ways. It seems very likely that he was the anonymous donor who in March 1909 promised a manse and a £100 stipend for a resident pastor. By the end of the year Mr Lewis was living in the manse, in Post Office Lane, next to the Oldfield's own home, Inglecroft. Mrs Oldfield gave a further endowment when her son returned safely from the First World War.

The second, external reason concerned the opening of St Peter's Mission Church by the Anglicans in January 1907. The *Cheltenham Chronicle* explained it thus: 'At all events it did not astonish one to find that this little tin church ran on interdenominational lines should fall very short of the ideal of many local Church people residing in the higher part of Bishop's Cleeve parish.' A new bishop in Gloucester seems to have instigated the venture.

The name St Peter's reflected the earlier chapel in Rising Sun Lane. As early as October 1901 the committee running the Convalescent Home had offered a site in their grounds for an Anglican chapel of ease, but the offer was refused. Not until January 1906 did Revd Thomas Jesson call together a small committee to consider the building of such a church. Led by W.M. Baker, a master of Cheltenham College who lived at Greystones at the bottom of the hill, the decision was taken to engage the Frazzi company, which had patented a hollow terracotta brick to give strength without weight, to make the best use of a sloping site near the Rising Sun. The final cost of around £550 was met by private subscription and a church grant. The building work was carried out by Amos Wilson and the interior was heavily influenced by the Arts and Crafts movement fashionable at the period. After it was opened, the congregations at the tin church fell, and their response was to appoint their own pastor. St Peter's, of course, was served by the parish clergy. Thus by 1914 the hill was served by two places of worship. Ironically the institution chosen to bind the community together had, in fact, split it into two, but the personalities involved had made their mark by being successful in a competitive environment, and it is not surprising therefore that this attitude pervaded their perceptions of community.

Another institution which Selina Jenkins mentioned on her visit in April 1903 was the golf course. This was an attraction for the residents and visitors but could not be said to have served as a community focus in the same way as that intended by the establishment of the places of worship. Rather we must understand it as another example of Cheltenham moving out of town on to the common land of Bishop's Cleeve.

There is no doubt the golf course originated in the wish of Cheltenham gentlemen to take advantage of Cheltenham's right to recreation on Cleeve Common as laid down by the 1890 Regulation Act. A public meeting was called at the Queen's Hotel in Cheltenham on 6 March 1891 with the purpose of setting out a golf course. Prestbury Park was soon dismissed as a potential course in favour of Cleeve Hill. The conservators negotiated an annual fee of £35 for the privilege; D. Brown of Malvern laid out the

The interior of St Peter's laid out for the Harvest Festival in 1910

course; and four rooms were engaged at Rock House to serve as the club house. In the Victorian age it seemed quite proper to allow lady members to be elected without allowing them use of the club dressing room, until improved accommodation was provided by the club house of 1895. This, in turn, was enlarged in 1904, when the club took over the whole of Rock House. To today's casual visitor to the common who is puzzled by the incongruous construction and style of the Youth Hostel, here is the answer – it was built at the turn of the century as a golf club house.

Cheltenham Golf Club was a club for gentlemen and their ladies. Membership was exclusive; the entrance fee four guineas; and the annual fee two guineas. A round of golf cost the visitor 2s. Ironically the residents on the hill, being only merchants and traders, could not join. Wealth could not buy status. As a result some of them met at Bayley's offices in the Promenade in Cheltenham on 12 February 1902. Called in its early days the Cheltenham Town Golf Club it entered into an agreement with the Cheltenham Golf Club and the Board of Conservators to play over the same course. Its first home was a wooden shed near Prescott Cottage, but this soon became inadequate and in 1905 a permanent club house was built on land next to the Rising Sun. Following later modification, this became 1 and 2 Cleeve Hill after the club moved out in 1937. Here the annual subscription was a mere 30s. and visitors could play over the same course as the gentlemen for only 1s. 6d. Our understanding of the development of the two clubs and their impact on the landscape has to be rooted in the class values of late Victorian and Edwardian society. When the caddying was performed by the locals, it confirmed their lowly status on their own territories.

Finally, there is one institution which Selina Jenkins did not mention – the Reading Room, built in 1893 by Henry Taylor as a place of improving recreation for the working classes. At his own expense he provided books, newspapers and games. We must not be surprised she failed to mention it, for by 1897 it had already closed. Why did it not survive his departure from the hill in 1896? The reason is not difficult to discover. He built it in the field bordering Wickfield Lane on Nottingham Hill, almost a mile from the growing settlement of Cleeve Hill. Our real surprise should be why he chose to build there, as he had already shown goodwill towards the residents by converting his laundry into St Peter's chapel in the much more convenient location of Rising Sun Lane. We will probably never know his reasons but at least someone seemed to be providing for the local working people whose traditional way of life had become so obviously swamped by the incomers during this period of rapid change immediately before the First World War. Whether they felt patronized or pleased is likely always to be another unanswerable question.

This view shows both the Interdenominational Church on the right and the short-lived Reading Room on the left horizon

The Quarries

The traditional life of the common continued under increasing pressure from the new demands of the early twentieth century. Not only did these include the burgeoning recreational use of the common, but also the increased quarrying activity which, again, brought some conflict between it and the communal rights for grazing. Again, also, there is a lack of detailed sources which tell the full story. As Selina Jenkins commented, quarrymen who worked in a 'quiet, genteel, any-time-will-do style' were unlikely to keep detailed records for future historians. Their scale was so limited that they were barely affected by recent legislation. The Quarry Fencing Act of 1887 ordered the fencing of all quarries lying within 50 yd of a public highway. No quarry fell into that category, which resulted in the Lords of the Manor considering they had no responsibility for fencing the quarries. In 1894 a Quarries Act required registration of all openworkings over 20 ft deep. Only one quarry was ever registered. Calling it simply 'Cleeve Hill', Arthur Yiend made the registration in March 1897, at which time he recorded the employment of two men.

The fullest record at any one time was made by the conservators in 1902 as they took on their responsibility for fencing the quarries. Stone was being

Wickfield Quarry was one of the last quarries to be worked. It is seen here in 1901. Now it is a car park [T.N. Curr]

A rusting reminder of quarrying. This winch still stands along the Undercliff at the top of a causeway of stone blocks. It dates from the last phase of exploitation around the time of the First World War [T.N. Curr]

extracted from Milestone, Ring, Sidelands, Hardstone, Freestone, Rolling Bank and Wickfield Lane Quarries in Bishop's Cleeve Manor. Only the first had adequate fencing. Gravel, mortar and sand were being taken from the King's Beeches where the Iron Age occupation site was discovered. Two unidentified sand holes were producing white sand, used in polishing marble and in making pottery. On Southam Manor, stone was being extracted from Cleeve Cloud, Freestone, Middle Hill and Postlip Quarries and gravel from the Middle Hill gravel pit. Most of these also needed fencing. From Captain Daubeny's book it is known that at this time Arthur Yiend was renting the rights to all the Bishop's Cleeve Quarries for £35 per annum. George Yiend was renting Southam quarries for £30 per annum.

The evidence in the landscape of this period of activity is no easier to identify than that for any other period. Apart from isolated digging of sands and gravels, all quarrying had ended within forty years, and grassed-over quarry faces tell no obvious tale. Even when lime was burnt it was done on

Gotherington station has now been restored to something like its original condition, shown here at the opening in 1906. Bishop's Cleeve station was of similar style but has now disappeared completely. Both were built by Arthur Yiend

the spot in temporary heaps mixed with coke under corrugated iron. However, some evidence does survive more clearly along the Undercliff above Thrift Wood. A causeway of large stone blocks leads from a rusting winch at the top to the overgrown foundation timbers of a wooden crane at the bottom – relics of an attempt to develop the quarry during this peak of pre-war activity. The crane broke on its second load, thus crippling the venture. It is said that Cleeve Cloud quarries were the only quarries where dynamite was used; at all the other quarries the stone was levered out with metal bars and sawn into blocks on-site.

Much local stone went into the building of the houses on the hill and keeping the local roads in some state of repair before the use of tarmac. Details of other uses are few, but their diversity is surprising. Arthur Yiend supplied stone for Cheltenham Ladies' College and for repairs to Tewkesbury Abbey. He built Bishop's Cleeve and Gotherington stations for the opening of the local railway line in 1906. He also supplied stone for work in Magdalen College, Oxford; Romsey Abbey; Winchester College; and for restoration work in several churches in what was then called Monmouth-shire. The difficulties of transport can be measured from his contract to

Recreational uses often supersede earlier economic activities. Castle Rock now serves as a popular rock climbing venue

A popular view of Cleeve Hill at the time of the First World War. Cheltenham Golf Club house is clearly visible to the left of the picture

CHELTENHAM CHRONICLE AND GLOUCESTERSHIRE GRAPHIC, SATURDAY, FEBRUARY 28, 1925.

COLMORE CUP OPEN RELIABILITY TRIAL.

On Saturday last the above Annual Competition was held over the usual course, Bushcombe Hill, a side road on Cleeve Hill, being the stiffest test in the whole ride. There were many failures.

1.—A competitor descending Post Office Lane.
2.—G. W. Walker (Sunbeam) at the Stopping and Starting Section in the middle of Bushcombe Hill.
3 and 6.—Part of the big crowd which lined the hill.

4.—B. Carter (Garfield) making a good ascent.
5.—W. B. Gibb (Douglas), of Gloucester, with a passenger, romped up.

7.—A skid while taking a difficult bend on Bushcombe.
8.—Miss M. Cottle, the famous Raleigh rider, was a competitor, and did well.

" Cheltenham Chronicle " Photos. Copies 1s. each, postage 2d. extra.

Scenes of the Colmore Cup Trials in 1925. It is too easy to forget the state of the roads before modern tarmac [T.N. Curr] supply stone for Besford Court, near Pershore. At one time thirteen teams of horses and a steam traction engine were employed. Such transport problems; the skill and increasing costs needed to extract the stone; and, above all, the availability of alternative materials, led to the abandonment of quarrying. It was responsible for the destruction of much archaeological evidence of earlier periods; it created a conflict of landscape use at least since the Roman period – not only by the quarrying itself, but by the multiplicity of trackways which caused injuries to grazing animals falling into the deep ruts; and yet it has given Cleeve Hill its character by which it is so easily recognizable from the vale today. In recent years it has provided for yet another use of the common, for the face at Cleeve Cloud has become a favourite venue for rock climbing; a new use for 'old' landscapes!

The End of an Era

By 1914 Cleeve Hill had been transformed from a small scatter of humble homes into a lively holiday resort and outer suburb of Cheltenham. It could cater for residents, long and short term visitors, and the day trippers. Many visitors came long distances and sent home a postcard or two with messages which provide valuable evidence for the historian. Many came on organized excursions.

At Whitsun 1910 an Esperanto congress was held here. It was claimed to have been the first public meeting ever held on the hill. A year later the National Deposit Friendly Society delegates came from their conference at Gloucester for an outing to the hill, using train and tram. The steepness of Gambles Lane led to Cleeve being made a stage of the Colmore cup motor trials before and after the First World War. These were run for motorcycles on a course around Birmingham, and Gambles Lane provided one of the hill climb portions of their trials.

However, the more significant activities on the hill in these years reflected the growing national concern with defence. The open space of the common has been used for many purposes during its long history; now it was to be used for military training. In November 1912 over two thousand members of the West of England Public Schools' Officer Training Corps took part in a 'battle' on the common in an exercise stretching from Andoversford to Bishop's Cleeve railway stations. A year later it was the turn of the OTCs of Birmingham and Bristol Universities to hold their field-day on the common. In August 1914 the First World War broke out, and the manoeuvres became for real. By the end of the year the 9th Gloucesters were marching up the hill every Wednesday for 'practising attacking exercises in open formation'. We know that such wave attacks became responsible for much of the mass slaughter on the Western Front by 1918. These soldiers were experiencing the end of an era. Many of them would be dead after the war, and life would never be the same again. On Cleeve the vitality and attractiveness of the Health Resort would never be recaptured.

FURTHER READING

Underpinning the detail of this chapter lie some of the books already mentioned in earlier chapters, i.e., the books by Hart, Blake and Beacham on Cheltenham; those by Daubeny and Garrett on Cleeve Hill itself. Contemporary published works have included Kelly's directories; Burrow's guidebooks to the 'Cotswold Health Resort' published from 1909; and volumes of the *Cheltenham Chronicle and Gloucester Graphic* (especially 1901 to 1903) which were issued as a weekly illustrated supplement to the *Gloucestershire Echo*. Copies of all these works can be consulted in Cheltenham or Gloucester Libraries. The latter also possesses a copy of a contemporary handbook for the Cheltenham Golf Club.

Much information came from the collections in the County Record Office: Cotswold Convalescent Home (HO 10 1/1), the interdenominational church (D4238), Bayley's catalogues (D4442), the building of Besford Road (DC/SJ57), and some items from Bishop's Cleeve parish council minutes (P46a PC1/1). Some of the records of St Peter's are kept in the vestry in Bishop's Cleeve parish church. Most of the deeds used still lie in private hands, and I am grateful to their owners for allowing me to use them. Similarly I have made extensive use of oral history in this chapter and exploited my own collection of pre-war postcards.

CHAPTER EIGHT

Postscript (since 1914)

Thousands of people visit Cleeve Common every year simply to
walk, ride or admire the scenery and views.
Gloucestershire Echo, 2 May 1988

The purpose of this book has been to investigate the development of a
landscape and identify themes within it. By 1914 the present appearance of
Cleeve, its common and community, had been created. Since that date the
changes which have occurred have generally reinforced these. This chapter
will concentrate on details not already covered to bring the story down to
the present; it is not intended to be a detailed history of Cleeve Hill in the
twentieth century.

Houses have continued to fill in the gaps between existing buildings.
Increasing planning restrictions since 1947 have forced new houses to reflect
the existing landscape. Nevertheless some of the atmosphere of the Health
Resort has been lost. The last tram ran in 1929. The Cleeve Hill café was
burnt down in the 1930s – all that remains are the overgrown terraces next
to St Peter's church. The building of the Geisha Tea House was demolished
during the writing of this book; a reconstituted Cotswold stone house now
fills its place. The tin church closed in 1972 as its congregation dwindled
and it lacked the greater institutional support which has ensured the
survival of St Peter's. It slowly crumbled as the land underneath subsided
until demolition in 1988. In 1979 the last post office, at Hilltop, closed and
it is no longer possible to buy a postcard of the hill in a shop on the hill. At
least one house, Samarkand, next to the tin church, has been built and
fallen down during the twentieth century as a result of land subsidence.
Phoenix House has recently risen on the site, refreshing memories of the
Health Resort by reintroducing balconies and verandas into the landscape.

Much has been lost, yet a great deal still survives. Not only the homes, but
the Malvern View and Rising Sun Hotels were joined between the wars by
the Cleeve Hill Hotel, which mirrored with its balconies the Geisha Tea
House next door. Many visitors now stay at the Youth Hostel. This has
ensured the continuing existence of the former golf club house, after the golf
club folded in 1936. It had already lost many members in 1922 when they

Samarkand literally fell apart as the ground beneath it slipped

The tramstop shortly after the last tram had run and the road had been tarmacked

broke away to form the Lilleybrook Golf Club on the other side of Cheltenham. The Cotswold Hills Club left their original club house for the existing club house in Wickfields in 1938, and then thirty-eight years later moved away to Ullenwood to enjoy an uninterrupted round of golf. The club house and course passed into the hands of Tewkesbury Borough Council who opened the Cleeve Hill Municipal Club. The conflict of interests thus continues, but there is a preference now to refer to 'management' of the common rather than 'conflict' on the common.

It might be a new word, but the problems it is trying to address are older than the common itself. Some traditional conflicts have disappeared. The decline in quarrying was outlined in the last chapter. A visitor in 1940 noted only Wickfields quarry in operation. Yet other conflicts persist. An interesting correspondence developed in the *Gloucestershire Echo* in the summer of 1982 which turned into a sheep versus golfers controversy, but this time the bulk of the letters supported tradition. In 1983 a sixth former from Cleeve School, Jill Clark, carried out an 'A' level study which identified thirteen conflicting interests held by visitors to the common. These ranged from walking, golf and horse training to model aeroplane flying, driving cars across the common and sheep grazing. At the Stockwell Lane entrance she identified eight conflicting uses in that one area. Problems of erosion, litter and degradation of the grazing were here at their most acute. Significantly, most people agreed with the quotation at the head of this chapter as the main reason for visiting the common. They were firmly opposed to any organized activities. Their perception of the common was that of quiet recreational space. They were, and are, heirs to the tradition of Cheltenham moving out of town.

The overriding concern of all formal and informal management schemes and proposals has been to keep the common as it is. It is very significant that the body elected to implement the 1890 Regulation Act was called the *Conservators*. Yet Cleeve Hill has always been subjected to people and forces which have altered and remoulded its appearance. Large areas have been destroyed by the same quarrying which today gives the bleak downland variety and interest. Since 1914 two strands of management are discernible: the national and the local. At times they have come together.

Today the rights of commoning are registered under the General Commons Registration Act of 1965. In April 1967, 1,332 acres were registered. Twenty-four commoners then registered their rights to common under the act. Their claims are limited to the numbers of animals their land in the vale can support in winter. However, if they all put their animals on the common between June and November we would then see around 3,050 sheep and lambs, 546 head of cattle, 58 horses, 8 goats and 3 donkeys. In practice, of course, sheep are the only animals regularly pastured because of problems of control and rustling. Under the Board of Conservators the responsibilities of the former hay warden's work has been divided into

Horse training remains an important use of the common. This photograph dates from 1935. It shows Lionel Densham riding Fieldmaster [B. Mustoe]

three: shepherding, regulating the use of the gallops for training, and enforcing the byelaws.

Much of the area of the common has been designated a Site of Special Scientific Interest to protect its rare flora from feet and trowels. For over twenty years Gloucestershire County Council has been working on a management strategy for the common, playing an updated role of the sixteenth-century Duchy of Lancaster court in trying to reconcile conflicting interests and to conserve and preserve the common's special features which are in danger of being destroyed by the people who come to enjoy them. It has worked with the Board of Conservators and Lords of the Manor, chiefly to regulate rights of way and resolve the problems of rights of free access; with the Nature Conservancy Council to safeguard delicate flora as the decline in grazing has led to the coarsing of the vegetation on the remoter stretches of the common; and also with the Tewkesbury Borough Council to provide interpretation and recreation facilities. An early result of this work was a report of 1971 which identified enjoying the view from the comfort of the car as the most popular pastime for visitors to the hill. Fifteen years later when the Borough Council proposed a picnic site and toilets at Stockwell Common, the inhabitants launched a campaign of local opposition. Like their nineteenth-century predecessors they, too, failed to prevent the incursion of outside influences.

This story of Cleeve began by considering the nature of common land and the problems of identifying clearly the rights attached to it; it closes by bringing the wheel full circle to this starting point. Despite legislation; despite management schemes; despite a century of the Board of Conservators, problems of rights and obligations are still complex and the origin of continuing conflict and confusion. Two examples can illustrate this. In May 1979 a small dog fell down a hole near Nutterswood. After four days of digging the dog was rescued; the police and fire officers departed; but who should back fill the hole? The conservators owned the rights to the minerals, which they had bought in 1957 for £200 together with sporting rights to

"Last time I was up here, I got hit by a golf ball —"

A fitting illustration with which to end. This recent cartoon reflects the continuing conflict of interests which has been a central theme of the history of Cleeve Hill [*Gloucestershire Echo*]

enable them to prosecute poachers, but they did not own the soil, which, in theory, belonged to the Lords of the Manor.

In the summer of 1985 a 'Rainbow Village' of two to three hundred hippies set up camp on West Down. The conservators had responsibility for enforcing the byelaw prohibiting the driving of vehicles across the common, but had no power to evict the hippies. The maximum fine they could impose was just 40s.! After lengthy legal discussions a court order was taken out by the Lords of the Manor who, as owners of the freehold of the common, were the only people who had the right to evict. This was done and the 'village' quickly disappeared.

This story has covered five thousand years, yet like any good story the end has yet to be written. During this time a landscape has been developed; it is possible to read that landscape for clues to its own history, to identify continuities, changes and conflicts, and within them three main turning points, in the Bronze Age, the later Middle Ages and at the end of the nineteenth century. In every age there have been some new developments but many of them are more usefully seen as old developments in new contexts. Cleeve Hill and its common is a fascinating piece of landscape, still very much a treasured resource in a crowded countryside. Those who visit it; those who live there; those who have responsibility for its future ought to be aware of its past. Increasing that awareness has been the ultimate purpose of this book.

FURTHER READING

Much further use has been made of the general works listed at the end of the Introduction. A fascinating glimpse of life on the hill can be found in *Gloucestershire Countryside* for April 1940. The register of claims to common land can be consulted in Shire Hall, Gloucester. The bulk of the chapter has been based on oral history and my own collection of local press cuttings made over the last twenty years. Local newspapers can be consulted in Cheltenham and Gloucester Libraries.

Acknowledgements

A work such as this could not have been written without the whole-hearted cooperation of a large number of people. Wherever possible I have already acknowledged them in the text and the captions. However, it has not been possible to thank in this way all who have helped me, and I gratefully acknowledge their assistance here. My research has taken so long that many might have forgotten their contribution, and several are no longer with us to enjoy the results of their help and advice. I apologize for any who might have inadvertently been omitted despite my careful recording of all the assistance I have received over the years.

Readers will already be aware that local records in the County Record Office have provided the backbone to this study. I thus start by thanking the County Archivists, Brian Smith and his successor David Smith, whose staff have dealt with many enquiries and requests with unfailing courtesy over many years. To the staffs at the other two major record repositories in the county, at Gloucester and Cheltenham libraries, I also extend my thanks. If my use of Bishop's Cleeve and Winchcombe libraries has necessarily been less, the assistance I have received there has been equally appreciated. Steven Blake at Cheltenham Museum has drawn my attention to the variety of material held there which has been relevant to this study, and I am grateful to him for that. Jackie Taylor and Tony Jones of the Planning Department at Shire Hall, Goucester, have provided information on the current plans for Cleeve Common.

Further afield, I wish to record my indebtedness to the staffs at the following repositories: Bodleian Library, Oxford; British Library, London; British Newspaper Library, Colindale; House of Lords' Record Office, London; Ordnance Survey (Boundaries Division), Southampton; Public Record Office, Chancery Lane, London; Worcestershire Record Office, St Helen's, Worcester.

I am indebted to Steven Bassett of Birmingham University and Professor Joan Thirsk of Oxford University for discussing some of the ideas in Chapters Two and Four respectively. Mick Aston of Bristol University has commented upon my manuscript, as has Christopher Dyer of Birmingham University, to whom I stand further indebted not only for allowing me to use his transcripts of the Bishop of Worcester's medieval court rolls, but also for accompanying me in search of the hidden medieval landscape. He also drew the plan of Wick.

Many local people, many of whom have known the area for far longer than myself, have given freely of their time and knowledge to fill in the gaps in the written record. I give my thanks to the following or their surviving relatives: C. Arno, T. Ballinger, P. Deakin, J.T.C. Denley, H. Gaskins, J. Garrett, E. Green, S. Hora, W. Humphries, A. Lunt, J. Mead, D. Oakey, G. Pitt, H. Smith, O. Stinchcombe, D. Waters, E. Way and W. Yiend. I am especially grateful to Vera Gardner, Vi Pearce and John Yiend who commented on the closing chapters to prevent my making too many obvious errors in my reconstruction of more recent events.

Just one person has been with this study since its inception. I have already acknowledged through the captions the enormous debt I owe to Tim Curr for his photographic work. But the debt is far deeper, for through four decades we have walked, talked and argued over Cleeve Hill, its common and its people. His continuing enthusiasm has been the necessary spur I needed to put the results in print. I hope he is not disappointed.

Finally, to my family, Margaret, Peter and Timothy for their forbearance and encouragement, particularly during the hectic recent months of turning notes into text, I once again give my thanks. The text itself has been transformed from illegible and confused manuscript to perfect typescript by Pat Freeth. She has cheerfully performed wonders in a very short time and no gratitude can be too great.

If any fault still remains after the help and advice of everybody listed here, I alone remain responsible.

Index of Places

No individual references are given for Bishop's Cleeve, Cleeve Hill or Southam.